Education of a Stranger
Storied-Poetic Words
for Threshold Crossings

SHOONIE HARTWIG

DEDICATION

for

JERRY
mpenzi yangu

CONTENTS

BARAKA (bahRAHkah)   *BLESSING*

The words behind the words. Blessing cannot stand alone. It is a circular weaving of Spirit giving and receiving, a binding, an interlacing from one to another. For those named within *baraka*, you have been the words behind my words. You have reflected Word Source in profound ways, bestowing a benediction on my living and my writing.

- To Kristopher and Rebecca, Kari and Dennis, Kurt and Lisa, and all my grands—it is your counsel, advice, and steadfast encouragement that sustain me—in all I do.

- To my editor-in-chief, son Kurt, you've questioned and prodded me every step of the way. Sometimes you've been downright pushy. I don't know where you get it.

- To son-in-law Dennis Murnyak, the tree cover is perfect.

- To readers Susan Thurston, Jamie Munson, Melanie Peterson-Hickey, Dalene Eimon, Bill and Rosa Small, Ludie and Fred White, Barbara and Bruce Nordstrom-Loeb, Janet Hagberg, Jodi Hanson, and Tim and Diane Sonnenberg. To Gerry Lidstrom's thoughtful editing during the early phases and to Larry Rasmussen and Daudi Msseemmaa in the later phase, your affirmation dared me to continue.

- To my two-hemisphere extended families—from Minnesota to Tanzania and North Carolina and in between, it is your lived words that sustain me.

- To Professor Mary Carlsen and the St. Olaf students in her "Ethics and Global Service" seminar in the fall of 2011, it is your questions for discussion that will challenge readers of this manuscript. Lauren Alvarez, Alana Anderson, Megan Andrews-Sharer, Holly Belgum, Christina Benjamin, Chloe Brennan, Amy Chatelaine, Julia Coffin, Amber Hesse, Chrisina Huntzinger, Benjamin Leis, David Matson, Emily Rosenberg, Michaela Roslawski, Sara Schaenzer, Brynna Schmidt, Josalan Sullivan, Bryan Wells.

- To my Mwangaza Family in Tanzania and all the US Volunteers, Board members, together we've been learning what it means to walk in the light of God. All proceeds from *Education of a Stranger* will go towards that continuing walk.

i

1 **VUMBUA** (voomBOOah)   n. *DISCOVERY*

Dictionaries are word travelers. When a word is defined and explained, its meaning is revealed. Yet the word sits there, on the page, all by itself. It's not until the word moves off the page, not until the word is used in configuration with other words, that its meaning comes alive. Only then can the particular shape of a word inform our interpretation through experience. As our vocabulary increases, there is greater certainty and assurance in our use of new word shapes because they have been born off the page into our known realities.

But when dictionaries translate words from one language to another, now that's another matter. A bridge is created between the known and the unknown. Unless you are a Swahili speaker, you probably don't know *vumbua*. Translating it from Swahili to the English word *discovery* makes sense. Now an English speaker can understand it, at least, as a word. But what happens when it moves off the page? What different interpretations might be discovered in an East African context that could reshape our initial understanding? Words are complicated.

Education of a Stranger is a word traveler, a story-filled lexicon that moves words like *education, hunger, books*, and *women and children* into spaces near and far where I have lived and discovered different understandings and new meanings. Whether I encountered them under a magnolia tree in North Carolina, or a baobab tree in Tanzania, these words have taught me definitions that go way beyond my earliest translations learned under a Norwegian fir in Minnesota.

To learn as a stranger is an educational discovery. To learn as an outsider, as an *mgeni,* when you don't belong, when your difference names you in a new space, this is where the possibilities begin. This is where words can reveal glimpses of new meanings, where surprising discoveries come wrapped around names and places.

Understanding is not as simple as word-for-word translation. There is a significant space between *vumbua* and *discovery.* This is where depth of meaning sits, waiting, waiting to be revealed by imagination and possibility. But there's no guarantee that a translation will emerge. Sometimes, the strangeness is so overpowering that we can't let go of our own words. Sometimes, we recognize only a loose connection because circumstances simply keep us at arm's length. Or, we enter a space briefly to get a sense of the environment and then leave. To stay in that space as a stranger requires courage and perseverance. But when others join us, others who bring their own words, that is when discovery midst mystery begins. That is when imaginations are fired as relationships are forged in a common cause. *Vumbua.*

I didn't have to go very far to discover this. When I was a teenager growing up in Northfield, Minnesota, I would walk across the Cannon River Bridge, the great divide separating the east from the west, to get to high school. My identity as a westsider didn't make any difference in my high school classroom. But a new reality awaited me when I was hired as a summer secretary by the Carleton College library.

When morning dawned that first day of work, I was really nervous. I took a deep breath as I pedaled my bike over the Cannon River Bridge and across Division Street. It wasn't only my green skills that concerned me. What would it be like over there? I was from the west side of the river in every way: Lutheran, with allegiance to St. Olaf College. In this midwestern version of Lake Wobegon, I knew where I belonged. How would they treat me in that alien territory, over there on the east side of the mighty Cannon? Suddenly, it seemed a long way from home.

My first task was to go into the basement and put the multi-year collection of the *New York Times* in order. After several hours of sorting through volumes of newspapers, I was puzzled because I couldn't locate the funnies. During coffee break, thinking I was addressing a serious issue of misplacement, I asked Mr. Richards, the head librarian, "Could you tell me where the funnies are in the *New York Times*, because they aren't included in the stacks you showed me."

There was this startled silence. And then, uproarious laughter. "Funnies. Did you say funnies?" he gasped. Everyone else joined in on a joke that I certainly didn't get. It was the beginning of good-humored fun and gentle mentoring that expanded my experience from the *Minneapolis Star and Tribune* to the *New York Times*. At the end of the first week, I pedaled home across Division Street, over the bridge, and up St. Olaf Avenue to Manitou Street, threw my bike on the lawn, ran through the front porch slamming the door, and yelled, "Hey Mom, they're really nice over there!"

Charlotte looked at me as if to say, "So? This is news?" As a member of the piano faculty at St. Olaf, she knew many music teachers at Carleton. She also joined professional women in a monthly dinner program which brought women together from both sides of the river. But she was old. I was young; this was a new discovery.

That was in the fifties, and I was a teenager. Now, five decades later, I am old, in my seventies. I'm still crossing rivers, still learning new words, still discovering. I continue to be a work in process, for my self-awareness is piqued whenever and wherever I am the outlier, the *mgeni*. This learning as a stranger has never been straightforward in its revelations. Paying attention isn't easy. But now I have the gift of retrospect. It is this reflective process that compels me to write *Education of a Stranger*.

What you will find in these pages are stories collected over a span of fifty years, stories of people and places who taught me well whether I was a teacher, wife, mother, project director, or volunteer. This lexicon with stories and poetry presents particular words that have reshaped my world since I left my early home and crossed over to Tanzania and North Carolina. These words have helped me pay attention whether entering new places or welcoming others into mine.

3

When I first went to Tanzania in 1960, my roles as a wife, a mother, a sometime teacher required my full attention. Daily tasks superseded any reflective time. Even though I continued to weave Tanzania into my landscape over the next forty years, it was not until I moved back to Tanzania in 1996 that the poetic reflections began to find life.

For seven years, I lived on Ilboru Road, outside of Arusha, Tanzania, all by myself. As a widow, as a mother with grown children, I moved there as a single, sixty year old missionary to facilitate educational partnerships between the twenty dioceses of the Evangelical Lutheran Church in Tanzania and their companion synods of the Evangelical Lutheran Church of America through Mwangaza Education for Partnership.

After three years of acclimating to my new roles and responsibilities with Mwangaza, poetry began to emerge, unbidden. The distractions of old were no longer present. Now, I was available to this space that dared me to stand before unknowns and shifting perspectives, daring me to enter mind-spirit contradictions. They were everywhere.

Several pieces are from Kwa Zulu, Natal South Africa. In 2003, I spent six weeks at the Pietermaritsburg School of Theology. The Iraq war declaration during that time became a cauldron of South African responses. I was in the middle of it as a white, U.S. citizen. It was a searing experience.

Dismantling assumptions and perceptions can be dangerous in writing yet the ever-present paradoxes that I had begun to know over the past forty years were finding word life. Throughout the discordant misery, throughout the compassionate possibilities, my soul has been and continues to be tethered to the unfathomable mystery.

As a two-hemisphere woman, I have two families – my children and kin in the United States and my Mwangaza family in Tanzania. They have given me the inexpressible gifts of love and encouragement in our living and in our learning together. Transformative resurrection takes practice as we seek to discover what is required of us so that all of God's creation might live abundantly. It is their accompaniment that has taught me.

Education of a Stranger is an education of the heart and soul. If my husband and I hadn't responded to an innocent piece of paper announcing the Teachers for East Africa program in 1960, I would have never learned "*Mahali ni pazuri*" in Tanzania. If we had not walked up the steps to Abiding Savior Church in Durham, North Carolina, in 1970, I would never have learned how to sing "Wade in the Water." The hymn I originally learned in Northfield, Minnesota, has not been forgotten, yet "A Mighty Fortress is our God" is not the only song that has meaning for me.

To the many who taught me how to sing new songs together, this two-hemisphere woman is very, very grateful.

Namshukuru Mungu.

2 **ELIMU** (ayeLEEmoo)   n. *EDUCATION, KNOWLEDGE*

If there is a commonality that threads its way through all our lives, it is education. We all know what it means to learn. My schooling as a stranger has been in and out of the classroom, in many places, with many teachers. How I have been taught, where, when, and by whom has given me a strange shape. And my learning is not over.

MALCOLM ~ ONESEMO

MALCOLM 1959

In 1958, my husband of three days and I embarked on a road trip from Minnesota to Massachusetts. Jerry and I knew nothing about married life. We knew nothing about Boston, to say anything of Harvard University. We grew up in small towns—Northfield, Minnesota, and Brush, Colorado. We'd studied music and history at St. Olaf College. Our commonalities were cornstalks, cows, our Scandinavian-German heritage, and the Lutheran Church.

At first glance, Jerry and Josh seemed an unlikely pair. As fellow students in the Master of Arts in Teaching program at Harvard University, they didn't appear to have much in common. However, within a few months, the casual, long-legged student from the other side of the Appalachian Mountains and the dapper African American from New York City discovered they were both outliers. The majority of students in their class were Ivy Leaguers. Josh and Jerry were suspect in regard to their intellectual abilities; they were also viewed as bereft of any cultural heritage.

The two became friends in and out of the classroom sharing meals in our sparse two-room Cambridge apartment. One evening, Josh asked, "Have you ever heard of Malcolm Little?" His question drew a complete blank. "Who?" we asked in complete ignorance.

Josh explained. "A debate is scheduled at Harvard Law School between Little and a lawyer with the NAACP. It could be interesting. With the civil rights movement and Dr. King's leadership, it might be a bit contentious. Little is Muslim. Want to go?"

"Why not?" we replied.

As we entered the law school building and climbed the worn steps to the second floor of the hall, we saw that many people were already gathered. We took our seats and began looking around. At each exit, a phalanx of young black men dressed in dark brown or black stood at attention, arms folded across their chests. Many men and women in the audience were similarly attired. There were few white folk.

It was not long before all seats were taken and late-comers crowded next to the wall. When the two debaters entered the stage, all exit doors shut. The attendant men stood in front of each, keeping their arms-across-the-chest pose. There was a low murmur in the crowd; an eerie sense of anticipation pervaded.

And then the tennis match of words began. First, the NAACP lawyer. The modulation of his voice was persuasive and conciliatory, his tones sometimes rising to a higher pitch and then backing away. This rhythmic pulse, this rising intonation and crescendo, I knew in music. Not in speech.

When Malcolm Little responded, the difference in modulation was electric. He spoke incisively, and though he, too, changed voice level, his intonation had an edge. It was pointed, not invitational. It was accusatory, not conciliatory. This angry discourse escalated as the debate continued. I was in the deep end of a swimming pool and the water kept coming up.

Words flew back and forth that were not in my vocabulary. Not only had I seldom heard them, I certainly had not articulated them. Like tennis balls lobbed over a net, the words shot between the debaters in rapid succession. Each man knocked inclusion-exclusion, integrate-separate, violence-nonviolence, Christian-Muslim with powerful rhetoric and precision. The Nation of Islam, Elijah Muhammad, Marcus Garvey, Uncle Tom, Martin Luther King, Jr. It went on and on. Hearing these words in this place, in this context, I realized my ignorance was profound. I could have been in physics class.

I felt a new strangeness, an increasing dis-ease. The repetitive angry accusations and strident tones of the debaters and the intensifying volume of response from the overwhelmingly black audience were knotting my stomach. At the conclusion of the debate, without hesitating a moment, Josh said quietly, "Let's get out of here!"

When I taught *The Autobiography of Malcolm X* to students at St. Olaf College twenty-five years later, this memory was uppermost in my mind because, in many ways, it was being replayed. The majority of students in my class had few reference points either in experience or in knowledge of how a Malcolm Little might become Malcolm X.

This was a man who knew no security in his home or in his community. By the time he was six, he knew violence from his father's death and hate from the Ku Klux Klan. He knew family dismemberment as he and his five siblings were separated and put into foster care. He knew a mother's breakdown because the avalanche of life events was too traumatic.

Education? Malcolm was a good student who demonstrated significant leadership skills. Yet his white teacher informed him that his aspiration to be an attorney was unrealistic for a "nigger." By eighth grade, Malcolm was a school dropout. By age twenty, he was in prison. He had become well schooled in street hustling, drug dealing, and burglary. The grammar of racial discrimination, hatred, and violence had translated into every aspect of his life.

Prison, however, became a transformative space. He read voraciously on a broad scope of subjects. He argued with fellow inmates about theology, western philosophy, about black consciousness, black freedom, and black unity. He became a sophisticated self-taught revolutionary, a convert to Islam, and an ardent follower of Elijah Muhammad. He developed a spartan self-discipline and a formidable work ethic.

8

Malcom's voice as a human rights activist became a powerful force advocating for all suffering and dispossessed people and naming racism as a primary contributor to their condition. When he traveled to Africa, his worldview changed dramatically. There, he witnessed people of different beliefs and heritage living together. It was a transformative experience. He became a revolutionary with a prophetic voice for all of America.

The making of an X. The meaning of a name.

THIS I KNOW

Subjugate
Diminish
Denigrate
Separate
Deny   **FOR THE BIBLE**
Pollute
Hoard
Devour
Pontificate
Demonize
Brutalize   **TELLS ME SO**

10

Minnesota ~ Massachusetts ~ Tanganyika

If you connect the dots on a map, it's a long way. In 1960, the flight took three days in a propeller plane. If I had thought it was a giant step from Minnesota to Massachusetts, it was nothing compared to the next leg of our journey.

Life after Harvard had continued in the Cambridge area as Jerry taught in the high school where he had interned as a student teacher. One chilly January day in 1960, he came home from school and with some enthusiasm said, "Guess what I heard at lunch today?" Not waiting for any reply, he continued, "There's a really exciting program out of Columbia University called Teachers for East Africa. Kenya, Tanganyika, and Uganda will soon be independent and they need teachers. Imagine. Africa!"

I was speechless. Dumbfounded. And I was not imagining. Okay, so we had talked about teaching abroad when we were first married, but that was over two years ago. Surely he couldn't be serious. Undaunted by my abnormal silence, he handed me a flyer. "Look! This explains it a bit more. And guess what?"

Again, there was no chance for me to respond since he carried on without taking a breath. "We would qualify given our college credentials and experience!"

He paused, I expect because my face was showing my response. Incredulity. Was he really serious? Somehow, I choked out, "WHERE?" As he stood by our kitchen table, I was nursing our two-month-old son, Karl, while twenty-month-old Kristopher played with his matchbox cars on the floor. Jerry had to be kidding.

Imagine Africa? I couldn't. My knowledge base was so small, it was impossible to conjure any sense of this new where. Jerry's persuasive ability, however, prevailed.

"Think about it," he said. "Africa. There'd be so much to learn!"

When I countered with, "But you said it's about TEACHING!" I got that look of raised eyebrows. Probably just as well that I let it go. I didn't have words. After many conversations, however, I agreed to at least apply. It seemed so unlikely we'd ever be selected that once the forms were mailed, I thought that would be the end of it.

By February, we were short-listed. Thousands of teachers applied from all over the United States, captivated with the possibility of teaching in an unknown environment amidst the beginnings of independence. By June, we were saying goodbye to family and friends, many of whom were puzzled, others startled, and everyone anxious. There was no precedent for what we were doing. We didn't know any teachers who took off for far-away lands. Nobody else did either. That included my mom, Charlotte, but she didn't miss a beat when we called her.

"If this is your sense of calling, go!"

What little we did know about East Africa was that mission work had been active there since the early 1900s as Catholics, Lutherans, and Anglicans established churches, schools, and hospitals. All 150 of the selected teachers were asked if we had preference for placement in a church related school. Tanganyika's long history of Lutheran relationships with Germany, Sweden, and America made it an easy choice.

By late July, we had not only entered a new hemisphere, we were beginning a new course in curriculum content and student population for which we had absolutely no preparation. Neither could have been imagined.

Ilboru Secondary School, located at the foot of Mountt Meru near Arusha, was our home and our learning place for the next three and a half years. This school, managed by the Lutheran Church, had achieved national attention for excellent examination results. We joined teachers from Canada, Norway, Great Britain, Tanganyika, and the United States. But there was nothing international about the required curriculum. Independence was only months away, but there were no plans for educational liberation.

British colonizers had left an indelible mark on secondary education. In addition to the requirement that English be the language of instruction, the curriculum used the same syllabus as schools in the United Kingdom and all other areas of Africa colonized by the British. The Cambridge examination at the end of Form IV, the senior year of high school, determined the subjects to be taught. Passing the Cambridge was the ultimate goal. Teaching for this exam and memorizing for this exam was the rule in all of Tanganyika's secondary schools.

Therefore, students studied geography of the Commonwealth, history of the Commonwealth, and literature of the Commonwealth, all in the language of the Commonwealth. Subjects reflecting the country of Tanganyika, the continent of Africa, its peoples, its politics, its history, and its environment were not included. Jerry taught British geography and history. I taught English or worked in the room of books that hoped to become a library.

Loliondo ~ Arusha

Loliondo, located on the northeast border of Tanganyika and Kenya, was home for Onesemo. It was a three-day walk to Arusha. Walking through parched savannah where there were no paths. Walking with a staff or spear where lions lurked. Onesemo Moyoi first trod this journey as a Form I student or ninth grader. He had already completed seven years of primary school, which was only a two-hour walk from his *boma* or home.

Onesemo had scored well on his Standard VII examination at the end of primary school, a feat of magnitude equal to his walk. When he started school, he knew Maa, the language spoken by his family and relatives, but his teachers used only Kiswahili in class. Crowded into a thatched-roof shelter, at least one-hundred youngsters crammed together, squatting on the dirt floor with slates in hand. No student ever held a book. If there was one, the teacher had it.

Students diligently copied information written by the teacher on a scarred blackboard. Questions were asked for group response. Depending on the teacher's English ability, most primary school students seldom heard it spoken, and few could read in this, their third language.

Onesemo had joined forty young men from all parts of Tanganyika when he took a coveted place at Ilboru Secondary School to begin Form I. In 1960, only 700 students throughout all of Tanganyika were able to attend secondary school. Ilboru Secondary School served 140 young men.

When we arrived at Ilboru, Onesemo was a Form III student, elected by his peers as head prefect. The majority of his classmates were our age mates. Many had not begun their education until they were eight, nine, or ten due to family needs. The fact that they had successfully passed examinations in spite of very rudimentary schooling indicated that they were exceptional. Their zeal to learn and their unstinting fervor to master information had interesting ramifications.

When a teacher entered a classroom, the scrape of forty-some chairs echoed off the cement floor as students stood with the formal greeting, "Good morning, sir!" However, if the students decided that the teacher was not teaching them well, they would strike. No scraping of chairs, no "Good morning, sir." There would be no students. It was a powerful tool. Their rationale? "We must pass the Cambridge! Our lives, our futures are at stake."

The students' determination to succeed was also apparent in their study habits. Lights out at 11:00 p.m. was strictly enforced by the teacher on duty. The two-story cement dormitories were crammed with teetering metal bunk beds that provided just the right cover for late-night readers. Hidden flashlights under the blankets extended study time into the wee hours of the morning.

The effects of this could be noted when students fell asleep in class or became ill. In desperation to curb this studying epidemic, students caught were assigned wood-chopping. This not only publicly declared, "Follow the rules!" it also exhausted them physically. It was a remedy that worked for some; others were incurable.

Onesemo, a tall, thin Maasai, was first in his family to study at the secondary level. As the elected leader of his fellow students, he also led his class in academic standing. Clearly he had figured out a studying pattern that held him in good stead.

The Maasai are nomadic herdsmen. They live in thorn-fenced circles or *bomas*. Their round mud-and-wattle homes with thatched roofs are spaced around the perimeter, leaving the center area as a safe haven where cows are protected from marauding night-time wildlife. Onesemo invited us to visit his home in December of 1961.

Sighting us from afar, he waved a welcome as our car teetered on a rutted trail that was intended for people or animals, not four-wheeled vehicles. In this flat landscape dotted with an occasional acacia tree, the red of the soil was the primary color. That is, until we could see his family standing and waiting. The women were attired in purples and reds. The *marani*, young warriors, were draped in red plaid *shukas,* or blankets. A stunning sight.

Greetings, always of primary importance, took a while. The traditional greeting, *habari gani*, "how are you?" not only acknowledges your presence, but also begins a process of establishing your identity. It moves from you as an individual to your family, "how are they?" thereby recognizing that you do not stand alone, ever. Just as the *boma* is a circle of several separate homes that belong together, it is this whole that names you. Your combined family members, their norms, and their life understandings form your basic identity, your grounding. This wholeness precedes your singular identity and names those to whom you belong. You are because family is.

Onesemo's father had four wives. His first wife was Onesemo's mother. Her ranking was important, as established by her occupying the first house next to her husband. This status in the *boma* included duty delegation to the other wives. It also guaranteed preferential opportunities for her children. When missionaries brought Christianity and education to this region, Onesemo's father accepted both on behalf of his *boma*. As a result, his first-born attended school.

Soon after our arrival, Onesemo's mama invited us into her home. The odor of farmyard dung followed us from the center of the *boma* and mixed with the smoky aroma from her wood fire. In this round room, only a small opening in the mud wall let in slivers of light. Three stones cradled a *chungu* or clay pot for cooking. *Chai*, a sweet tea with sugar and milk, was offered. It continues to be the hospitable offering in any home. Sipping, talking, and story-telling transformed these simple, plain surroundings into a space of gracious warmth.

As we prepared to leave, Onesemo's mama took my hand and walked me to where several *kibuyus,* or gourds, were propped against the wall. These beautiful, long, slender gourds were decorated with burn patterns. Each had an attached leather strap, studded with beads in the preferred Maasai colors of reds, blues, and whites, to make it easy to sling over your shoulder.

Onesemo translated as she showed me a removable cap, not unlike a nipple, on one of the gourds. She explained that milk could be kept in it for your baby when you were out with the cows and had little time to nurse. Then she placed it in my hand with gratitude for nourishing her son in a far-away place, distant in every conceivable way from her home. Her *kibuyu* continues to hang on my living room wall.

Onesemo graduated from Ilboru Secondary School later that month. When we returned to Cambridge, Massachusetts, three years later to collect our stored possessions, we met him in Harvard Square for tea. His study habits had served him well. He was in his second year at Harvard with a dream of medical school. It happened.

Today, he is ranked at the top of his field as a researcher of East African cattle diseases. Other graduates from Ilboru Secondary School are peppered throughout Tanzania and many international organizations as professors, writers, and government and church leaders. Their names read like a Who's Who.

ISAIAH

"The Lord God has given me the tongue of those who are taught
That I may know how to sustain with a word
Those who are weary
     Morning by morning you awaken me
     You awaken my ears
     As those who are taught"

               ISAIAH
               My main man

I thought Chapter 43 said it all

     "Though you walk through fire-"
        You know that part and
        He ends it

     "I call you by name
        You are mine."

It's perfect
     The imagery
        The deepest knowing
        of
               Fear
                  And

               Belonging

And then the wellspring
     Of God's might
        Knowing and claiming
               Me

     "I call you by name
        You are mine."

Now these verses from Chapter 50
     Unbidden
        Capture me
            In a deadlock grip

Oh Isaiah
   Tell it
   Tell it to us who need to hear it
Because we have been taught
   God knows we have been taught

      To read
      To write
      To compute
      To negotiate
      To litigate
         And yes

      To
      Discriminate

What words have we
   For the weary
      The weary of spirit
      The weary of body
      The weary of mind

What have we been taught?

      I Remember

To love our God with all that is within us
   To love our neighbor
      As
         Ourselves

If my tongue has been taught
What words have I
      To turn despair to possibility
      To restore safety where violence rages

What ways are there to show my love
   In my excess
   In my indifference
   In my arrogance

What paths can I walk
    To teach me
        What injustice looks like

      Midst

   The abandoned

   The unseen

   The unheard

   The unwanted
        What paths can I walk
          To show me
            Where God's love is known
        Midst

        Mud and wattle homes
        Death of too many children
        The wandering homeless

I can't do it alone
    Show me
        Tafadhali

    Teach me

How your weariness erupts in song
    How your gratefulness is boundless
    How your tongue confesses

      God is God
        of
        All

So that I, too, can awaken
    With your words
      To ease
        My   weary   soul

3 **WAPI** (WAHpee)   adv. *WHERE, PLACE*

If where is a question, which it usually is, sometimes you know the answer. Sometimes not. Somewhere doesn't tell you much. Everywhere, well, okay, but could you be a little more specific? Wherever is so noncommittal that it tells you nothing. And the ultimate is nowhere. All have to do with this elusive word *wapi* which hides powerful emotions. Every *where* continues to teach me wherever I go.

Arusha ~ Northfield

ARUSHA **1961**

You need to watch out for *wapi*. A small, simple word if you ask where to go to lunch, shop, or vacation. But once you take *wapi* out of your own setting, there's absolutely no guarantee where it might take you.

Soon after our selection by Teachers for East Africa in May of 1961, we were informed of travel, orientation, and placement details. Jerry flew in a prop plane as one of the 150 selected teachers for a six-week orientation at the University of Makerere in Kampala, Uganda. I followed with our two small sons in late July. Lutheran personnel in Minneapolis had contacted us earlier regarding a placement with a Lutheran-managed school in Tanganyika. Columbia University officials then informed us that we would be given our specific assignment at the end of orientation. A plan.

Within a week of my arrival in Uganda, all of the 150 teachers were assigned to secondary schools in Uganda, Tanganyika, or Kenya. All, that is, except the Hartwigs. The only explanation offered by a Columbia representative was that they had not received a specific school designation for us.

20

The explanation sounded like this: "We have a solution for you. You will be in Tanganyika. But where, we don't know. We contacted Lutheran personnel in Moshi and informed them that you are coming – by train. Surely they will know what to do with you."

We were going nowhere by train? We could have walked faster. For two days, we watched in amazement as a new world unfolded outside the dusty train windows—parched red soil, filigree of acacia trees, bedraggled children herding goats and cows, hordes of people at each station speaking rapidly in an unintelligible language as they hawked peanuts and fruit. We were overwhelmed by this world of unknowns as we tried to cope with sick, tired kids in a very cramped space in the days before Pampers, with little food that made any sense to our taste buds.

When we arrived in Moshi on the slope of Mount Kilimanjaro, our welcoming committee was small. We were summarily ushered into an office where one man with a German accent said, "We have no room for you here! But if you will wait, I'll call the headmaster at Ilboru Secondary School near Arusha. Maybe, maybe they can accommodate you."

As we waited, we could hear his raised voice from the next room. "We have TWO Americans here with TWO children who have just arrived. We have NO position. We have no room."

Returning to us, smiling happily, he said, "We will find a taxi for you and you will be driven to Arusha. Actually, they don't need teachers either, but you can go there for now."

The *wapi*, the where of this endless journey wasn't our only question. Why had we ever thought this was a good idea? Two parents, two babes, two suitcases. Survival mode took over. Again. We tucked ourselves into a taxi, the vehicle chosen to transport us to somewhere. Our driver spoke no English; we spoke no Swahili.

The drive between Moshi and Arusha took close to three hours. The rutted road, the sudden swerves as we veered between potholes, and the raucous rattling of the taxi caused us to hold onto our boys, tightly. And then, suddenly there she was, Mount Kilimanjaro, erupting from the plains in snow-covered glory. The simplicity of the surrounding landscape, the scrub brush, red clay soil, and herdsmen tending cows and goats only added to the magnificence of this more than 19,000 feet of mountain splendor.

You could say the sight took my breath away. Actually, my breathing was already shallow. It seemed like my head was saying to my body, "I dare you to inhale!"

As we approached Arusha, we could see the town in the distance, but our driver chose another road, a dirt track lined with scantily boarded shacks, precarious tables offering bananas, tomatoes, and onions. Where was he taking us? There had been little traffic on the Moshi-Arusha journey. A few trucks, a few cars. A lot of cows.

But on this road, people were the traffic. Women perched on low stools, fanning a charcoal fire where corn roasted. Women stood by their produce, talking with all the passers-by. Children barefoot, running back and forth. Men in suits, talking with friends. Women in smart outfits and high heels, laughing, chatting. Old women, barefoot, wrapped in colorful cotton cloths, moving slowly. Cows and goats meandered, bicycles careened. Everyone, everything, in the middle of the road.

When we finally turned into a large field, rumbling to a stop, the driver leapt out to assist us. Two parents, two babes, two suitcases. He said something, shook our hands, got back in his taxi and rattled off.

We looked around. In and around this open space, cows grazed. Strange-looking tree stalks with furled green leaves surrounded the field. The only people in sight were young boys kicking a makeshift ball. My quizzical look to Jerry got this response: "Soccer."

A soccer field? This was it? Past feeling, past words, past weary, past fear, I picked up Karl and one suitcase, following Jerry with Kristopher and the other suitcase. A roof peeked above trees in the distance. Some where.

It isn't always easy for those who watch and wait for those who are discovering.

A month before my third birthday on a hot, dry July day in Iowa, my dad suffered a massive heart attack. He never recovered. Normal changed forever. And with it, the where of our family in residence and in identity was never the same. It was 1938. The Depression had hit hard in Story City. The two-family shared ownership in a Ford car dealership couldn't sustain us. Not without my dad. My sisters, Peggy and Betty Ann, were studying at St. Olaf College. My brothers, Jack and Gus, were in the ninth and fourth grades.

Before the end of July, my mother, Charlotte, received a telephone call from F. Melius Christiansen at St. Olaf College. He remembered her from her student days, but he also knew my sisters as singers in the St. Olaf Choir. He offered her the possibility of teaching piano at the college. Six weeks later we left our home, our car, and all of our relatives. Charlotte left her home in Story City, the gracious two-story, wrap-around-porch place where she grew up, where she birthed me, where she had welcomed her husband home every evening for twenty-two years, where sisters, nieces, nephews, church, and school surrounded her.

In Northfield, we rented a modest two-story, white frame house where my sisters, Charlotte, and I shared one bedroom, and my brothers slept in a closet-sized alcove next to the washing machine. Upstairs rooms were rented to male St. Olaf students.

Everyone was always leaving. "Where are you going?" was my continual question. Everyone had an answer except me. And everyone left, except me. I quickly learned that waiting could be boring.

The Odd Fellows Home, a retirement home for war veterans, was next door. Spreading oaks and elms shaded a lawn with two-seater framed swings. An invitation. After everyone left, this became my regular waiting place because I had a friend, Billy, an Odd Fellow. It wasn't just the swing or his stories that fascinated me, it was his peg leg. My grandfather could move his tongue to loosen his dentures, and his repetitions never ceased to amuse me. But a peg leg? Absolutely fascinating.

One day, probably mid-afternoon, Billy developed a thirst. His invitation to walk downtown for a drink seemed better than swinging and waiting. Off we went, hand-in-hand. It was a memorable, halting walk. We were a pair. Billy in a plaid shirt with suspenders holding up his brown, scruffy pants and me in my favorite blue pleated skirt and white blouse. My hair was undoubtedly done in the usual sausage curls with a big bow. Billy's balding pate would have made a singular contrast.

Upon our return a good hour or so later, it was to find a frantic mother searching for me. "Where, WHERE have you been?" she cried. "Oh," I replied, quite nonchalantly, "Billy and I went to the bar so he could have a beer."

4 **MAZINGIRA** (mahzeenGEERah)   n. *ENVIRONMENT,*
SURROUNDINGS

Growing up in southern Minnesota, I translated that known environment into a template through which I made sense of my surroundings and ways of living wherever I was. That geographical setting, the people, the places, was my norm. This was where I belonged. When I left Minnesota, however, I didn't leave it behind. It accompanied me. It wasn't only the outer landscape that would teach me. As profound was the interior of my soul.

Arusha, Tanganyika   **1961-64**

The southern hemisphere. We were on a fast experiential learning curve. Some aspects were easier than others. For two weeks after we were dumped in the soccer field, we lived inside unspoken, anxiety-filled questions: "Will we find a school where they need a teacher? And, if not, then what? Where will we go?"

There is a quality of time in this hemisphere that defies schedules. There is elasticity with any response to when that will drive northern hemisphere folk absolutely crazy unless you can reconcile yourself to not knowing the answer, yet feel sure that whatever you're waiting for will happen. Sometime.

And it did. Within two weeks of crouching inside the question mark, we began to stretch, albeit slowly, to an exclamation point. Due to family and health issues, two teachers suddenly resigned at Ilboru Secondary School. Our where and when were answered. We would stay. We were needed!

The school was only a five-minute walk from the notable soccer field where we had unceremoniously entered the Ilboru village. It took a half hour or so to walk to Arusha town, a bustling city, gateway to Serengeti Game Reserve and Ngorongoro Crater. In the village, we lived at a much more leisurely pace. Mount Meru, soaring to 14,980 feet, greeted us with her sharp, slate-grey outline on a clear day. Bougainvillea, jacaranda, fir, and banana trees colored our view everywhere.

When we arrived in August, the temperatures were a surprise. During the day, seventy degrees and sunny meant short-sleeved shirts. At night, however, we slept with blankets. When morning dawned, fifty-five degrees was downright chilly. No wonder there were fireplaces in some homes. Our house didn't have one. We did have a breezeway of sorts, our dining area. At breakfast, we held hot mugs of coffee or cocoa for hand warmth, the rest of our bodies layered with sweatshirts and shivering. We didn't have enough warm clothes, but within six weeks, my mom had mailed snuggly pj's for our boys. The tropics?

We were accustomed to four seasonal changes; Minnesota had done a good job of that. Arusha, however, taught us two: dry and wet. The big rains usually came in February and lasted into May. We would discover that "big rains" meant just that. A lot of wetness, like fifty-five inches a year. The high clay content in the soil made for very slippery walking and driving. During those months, it gradually became colder and colder, requiring layers to stave off the sixty-degree damp chill.

By September, a more tropical climate returned with the dry season. You could depend on the sun for the day; clothes dried outside, all the time. Now, the temperatures gradually heated up. By January, if you lived in coastal regions or in lowland areas, you definitely knew you were in the southern hemisphere, sweating in ninety-plus degrees. But in Arusha at 4,000 feet elevation, even during the dry season's heat of high eighties during the day, evenings were never unbearable. A very livable climate.

Mazingira. The environment of a day was as new as the seasons. It always began before dawn's break with strident cocks' crows from our neighbors' yards, mixed with melismatic chanting from the town mosque. But by seven o'clock, dawn was well cracked, the day fully awake. And so was our world with people walking, cars honking, children running. For twelve hours, light illumined life. Seven o'clock. Darkness returned. The southern hemisphere sky so bright, so close, you could imagine reaching up and touching a star.

When night descended with its jet-black cover, daytime sounds diminished to a murmur. A bush baby's cry or barking dogs interrupted the enveloping comfort we felt when under our blankets. Erratic electricity required that flashlights and candles be kept in arm's reach. Night time. Long time.

Polepole describes Tanzanian time. It means easily. It means slowly. It means like night and day, not in a hurry. This life rhythm was embedded in an environmental process of connecting. Much happened and nothing happened in a day. The *hodi*s at our door were constant. Without doorbells, *hodi*, the call from a visitor, asked, "Is anyone home?" A mama selling eggs, a child delivering milk, a teacher needing a ride to town. By day's end, reflection on what occurred was always so varied, so full, and yet the answer to, "What did I do today?" was not measurable.

During those early months at Ilboru, I paid a lot of attention to many matters of health. I knew about preventive health measures as a young mother. In the states, I'd take my boys to the doctor regularly to be immunized against polio, diphtheria, whooping cough, and tetanus. A pediatrician's office could be found when fevers or falls or interesting rashes appeared. Between Dr. Spock and doctor visits, I felt confident in caring for my young ones. But here, in this new environment, *mazingira* offered little buffer, little space between us and a multiplicity of biological hazards.

In Tanganyika, in this new environment, protecting my family's health wasn't that simple. If I didn't boil water, we could get typhoid. If I didn't boil milk, delivered straight from the cow in a beer bottle with a tobacco plug, we could get salmonella. If I didn't scrub vegetables well, we could get dysentery. If the boys ran barefoot, they could get worms.

Then there was the ubiquitous mosquito challenge. We slept under nets and took prophylactics for malaria. Yet I was hospitalized twice. We also had a snake-bite kit in the refrigerator with anti-venom serum just in case. Yes, black mambas were present though I never saw one. The possibilities for not being well were everywhere. After several months, however, we had established a routine that moved these daily precautions from unusual to ordinary. Within a day, that changed.

Next door to us lived a young Tanganyikan family. Gilbert taught science at Ilboru. He and his wife, Naomi, would proudly bring their infant daughter, Sarah, to school celebrations. One morning, I awakened to wailing like I'd never heard. It was an avalanche of blinding sorrow, a raw cry that swept beyond their compound and hurtled into everyone's yard. Running outside, I asked another neighbor, "What has happened? Why are people crying?"

Emmanueli looked at me, sadness etched into the lines of his worn face. "Last night, baby Sarah was crawling, she was eating, she was happy. But this morning, she is no longer living."

Stunned, rooted to the spot, I could not move. I had heard her sweet, six-month-old voice chirping in the back yard only yesterday afternoon. I stumbled back to our house. There was terror in my heart. If this happened to Sarah, what about my dear hearts Kristopher and Karl?

The terror did not subside because there was no escape. Within hours, a carpenter was working nearby. We could hear every pull of the saw as he hewed boards out of tree limbs. The sound was a drone that became a dirge. But it was the rhythmic drumming of the hammer securing nails into her small box that would awaken me from my dreams and bring terror to my heart for years. Not a cradle to rock, not a crib to shelter, but a wee coffin for Sarah.

The day of her service dawned. All of our school and nearby community gathered to sing and to pray. At the gravesite, we each took our turn to lay sprays of purple, white, and orange bougainvillea branches amidst the clumps of red earth on Sarah's grave. The cause of her death remained a mystery. Perhaps it was Sudden Infant Death Syndrome. Perhaps it was a sudden malaria attack. We would never know.

What we did learn was the ever-present reality of death's rawness, its inescapable presence in the midst of life. Like the seasons of wet and dry, the rhythm of night and day, life and death crashed into our environment with a force reaching beyond a child's sudden death. It was woven into the *mazingira*, the environment, the inextricable linking of all nature's forces that could not be denied, could not be separated or hidden. Seamless.

HIDDEN FACE

Hide not your face from me
It is everywhere in the Psalms Isaiah Jeremiah
Abandoned
Rejected
Hopeless
Desperate

WHERE ARE YOU? cry prophets God's people
Through the ages
Then there is Job

And here
It's in MY face
I can't get away from the hiddenness of you

Mama
Help my son   See his stomach
Look at his legs
Distended swollen
Mama
Help my daughter
We have no school fees
She's doing so well
But the crops

Mama
My husband left me
Six children
No support
No food
No work

I'm drowning in your absence
I'm overwhelmed with starkness of need
I'm angry
I'm tired

No escaping
    Sadness
        Hopelessness in sickness
        And in health
Overwhelming odds for survival
    Children
        Abandoned
           Dying

No escaping
    This everyday reality
        Living on the edge

So
    I rant
        I complain
No escaping
    The hiddenness of you
        If only there was a distance
           If only a comfortable space
So that
    I

        Could hide
           From those in gnawing hunger
           From the desperateness
                breeding cunning and deceit
           From misshapen bodies of need

Where to hide
    From the least of these sacrificial ones

Which question?
    Where are you?

    Where are we?

Wading in the water

5 **LUGHA** (LOOgah)   n. *LANGUAGE*

Linguistic fluency wasn't in my background. English was sufficient. Charlotte insisted on Proper English. Grammar mistakes were always corrected. Slang, and heaven forbid four-letter words, would be cause for an Ivory soap mouthwash. Entering a new language world in Tanganyika required more than translation of literal meanings. Expressions of heart, soul, and body had their own language. There was no dictionary.

Tanganyika ~ South Africa

TANGANYIKA 1961

The swirls of language sounds captured my ears from the day we arrived in Tanganyika. The rhythmic flow of Swahili is so beautifully cadenced that your ear responds to its lilt even if understanding is absent. Try this: *Nataka chakula* (nahtahkah chaKOOla). I hope you're hungry because it means "I'd like food."

In Swahili, the vowel phonation never changes: 'a' is ah, 'e' is aye, 'i' is ee, 'o' is oh and 'u' is oo. Furthermore, the emphasis on the next-to-the-last syllable never changes. The result is a language that rolls off your tongue. But it wasn't only Swahili in the sound mix. With 120 distinct ethnic groups throughout the country, that translated to 120 different languages.

As we were living in the Maasai region, what I was often hearing was not Kiswahili but KiMaasai or Maa. The "ki" preface, by the way, denotes linguistic identity, but it is often not used. My first teachers were mamas who came to my door selling eggs, onions, and tomatoes. Their first language was Maa. But they were kind and only engaged me in Swahili. Armed with a *Teach Yourself Swahili* book, I experienced these tutorials in the context of daily life.

Advent in Tanganyika. 1961. Hot, dry, dusty. Poinsettia bushes surrounded the gate by our house. Some were eight feet tall, luxurious in this arid season. Deserts shall blossom? Sounded and looked Biblical. The luxuriant red petals were full of themselves. It was the only connection to this season as I'd known it, never mind that our poinsettias in the states were pitiful in comparison.

Yet I soon discovered another. Someone heard that I loved singing, probably because I joined the village church choir. When I received an invitation to sing, however, it was not with a choir but to participate in a church dedication up the slopes of Mount Meru. In some places, singing by yourself is called a solo. But here? I hadn't heard one yet.

Here, everyone sang by heart, everyone harmonized. At the Ilboru church there was no need for the pump organ, which was just as well. Daudi, an elder in our congregation, was trained by German missionaries in the 1940s. He had HIS tempo, yet our Ilboru congregation sang, in a word, slowly.

This invitation to sing by myself had me spooked, scared, nervous. My friend Rispah, a Maasai woman, told me it would be good to sing in Maa. We had only been in Tanganyika five months. My faltering Swahili was pitiful and my Maa nonexistent.

"Don't worry," she said. "I'll teach you."

She began to sing these strange words: *sidai, sidai esipa.* At first, the sound was unintelligible. But gradually, as I let the tune enter my ears, I was astounded. I knew it! Back in Minnesota, "When Christmas Morn is Dawning," this same hymn, we sang during Advent. How did it get here?

It didn't take long to find out. This tune accompanied German missionaries to Africa in the early 1900s, along with other hymns, liturgy, and their understanding of Christianity. One of the first American Lutheran missionaries in this region, Dave Simonson, was the one who invited me to sing. Dave's work building churches and helping to establish hospitals and schools was just beginning.

The Sunday of the dedication dawned with the usual startlingly blue, clear sky providing the setting for Mount Meru's soaring height in the background. We drove up the lower slopes slowly. As we approached the church, it was not the construction that caught our attention. It was the sea of vibrantly clothed people, *khangas* (patterned cotton shawls) and *shukas* (draped blankets) everywhere. Maasai warriors were draped in bold orange plaid. Women were wrapped in purple and magenta, all ready for a celebration.

When we got out of the car, mamas swarmed around us, arms out-stretched, an invitation to hold the boys. Kristopher stood with his legs firmly planted on the ground, resisting any attempts to lift him up by holding tightly onto his dad's leg. An anchor in the sea.

Karl, however, was immediately swept out of my arms into the crowd and handed from one mama to another. His whiteness was clearly a source of curiosity to all. People crowded closely, touching his skin, his hair, pointing at his blue eyes, then looking at one another, laughing with gusto. If they were amazed, so was Karl. At first, he too looked at everyone with interest but then his little body started to stretch, searching the sea of faces for familiarity. We weren't hard to find.

When we entered the church, it was already full. One side for men, the other side for women. Another German tradition. The benches were crammed. The white-washed cement walls were lined with people standing wherever a space could be found. Outside, people were shoving to get a place near a window, close enough to peek from the outside in. Jerry stood at the back, Karl in one arm, Kristopher still holding onto his dad's leg and standing as tall as he could. As for me, I was ushered up to the front. Quaking.

Once the service began, I felt some familiarity. The liturgy inherited from the Germans I knew from our Ilboru church. But then the moment came. The pastor stood up and proceeded to explain my presence. He told everyone that there was this mama who was going to sing, BY HERSELF, so would everyone just listen, please.

My heart was hammering so loudly, couldn't they hear it? Necks craned around the window ledges, hundreds of eyes peering at me. With quavering voice, I began. *Sidai, sidai esipa.* Eyes widened in astonishment and then recognition, and then the smiles. Ah, the wonder of what that does to the face. The sun shone inside.

Before I had finished the first phrase, I could hear, yes, and feel, sound coming towards me. From the back of the men's side a murmuring. Faces alert, piercing eyes focused on this *mzungu*, this white mama singing. Alone? Not possible. As I began the second phrase, *teni kiataa pokin*, the sound was moving closer and closer. I was engulfed by a warm musical wave that encircled me as the women gradually joined in. My voice took courage and I sang with my whole heart in the midst of this glorious chorus.

Sidai, sidai esipa in Maa, *Mahali ni pazuri* in Swahili continues to be the binding hymn throughout Tanzania. This tune of German heritage has been transformed into words that are grounded in this place. "There will be a beautiful place, where all of us will stand in the same *boma*, in the same circle of homes, where there is one tribe, there is one Shepherd of us all."

I continue to discover what it means to be lost and found in translation.

THE SOUTHERN CROSS

We are often troubled
Dispossessed
Compassionate
Impoverished

But never crushed

Ngoma

Sometimes in doubt
Wandering
Mourning
Singing

But never in despair

Ndota

There are many enemies   *But we are never without a friend*
Greed   Wounded
Brutalality   Compassion
Hope   Silenced

Mystery

And though badly hurt at times
Raped
Killed
Forgiving
Demeaned

We   The
Are   Stars
Not   Always
Destroyed   Shine

Ngoma dance   **Ndota** star
II Cor: 4:6   SH: 4-6

"Onward Christian soldiers, marching as to war with the cross of Jesus, going on before." I first sang this hymn at St. John's in Northfield. But it can be heard on a Sunday morning in churches throughout the U.S. and beyond. The imagery of violence together with a cross invokes a very different sentiment than *sidai, sidai esipa*. War. *Vita.* I knew the word from a distance. It is such a small word yet so monstrous, so huge in reality, so violent in its multitudes of translations.

The African continent bears deeply entrenched war tread marks. Rwanda, Congo, South Africa, Uganda. Their very names call to mind one word—war. *Vita.* These countries neighbor Tanzania. Within their borders, conflict has had another naming, civil war. Yet this infection has not spread into Tanzania. Independent since 1964, Tanzania is the only country in sub-Saharan Africa without civil war as part of its history. It is a stunning legacy of peace-keeping that few countries in the world can match.

How does any group define itself? Who belongs? Who is excluded? Who can? Who can't? Tanzania's answer has been this: We are. The 120 ethnic groups in Tanzania do not deny their particular heritage. Yet there is no dominant ethnic group in leadership or in resource control. There is a national language that fosters cohesion. There is a relatively equal mix of Muslim, Christian, and traditional believers who are intertwined in families, in positions of authority, in ownership. There is a constitutional presidential selection process that alternates Christian and Muslim believers. Peaceful memory has been and is being shaped.

We are. For years, I had heard about apartheid. When I was teaching at St. Olaf in the eighties, we welcomed many students from Namibia, a country then governed by South Africa which did not offer higher education to Namibians. We held anti-apartheid rallies and divested from South African companies. We offered scholarships. From a distance, along with multitudes of others, we lifted our voices and shut our pocketbooks in solidarity.

Then we began to hear the stories. Nelson Mandela. Bishop Tutu. Steve Biko. Soweto. And the world was brought to its knees as war memories were transcended by those who refused to let its sins shape their future. Changes were happening. Barriers were crumbling and reconciliation and forgiveness had new translations. I wondered and marveled from afar.

Many of our Tanzanian church leaders had enrolled at the University of Pietermaritsburg in the Kwa Zulu Natal province of South Africa. They studied theology. With apartheid memory, with institutional separation by color, with Biblical interpretations of right and might, how would issues of difference and identity be addressed within a seminary context in 2003? How would memory transcend in scriptural translations, in development and women's studies, in global health and the increasing presence of HIV/AIDS?

I arrived in Pietermaritsburg in March of 2003. The German couple who managed the Lutheran seminary hostel, guest house, and library had made the necessary preparations for my six weeks' stay. I would be the only scholar in residence in the modest, very adequate guest house. The amenities of stove, refrigerator, running water, good lighting, electrical outlets, table, chair, privacy in bedroom and bath had all the earmarks of study and living space conducive to learning and writing.

The seminary, located right on the university grounds, was impressive. The beautifully constructed dark red brick buildings bore a European gothic air of hallowed, grand space for those selected, those especially intelligent learners. Established by and for Afrikaans, the ivy-covered walls, the cathedral-like halls, the lush coiffured grounds brought attention to the grandeur of a place created for exclusive learning.

Coloreds, whites, and blacks. The color line enforced by brick and mortar. Historically, each group had its separate campus. With the fall of apartheid, changes were still fresh in the making. It took a while. What had been, seemingly, ordained by God, was now in a new incarnation. This university had been all white in student and faculty presence. By 2003, change was apparent. Most of the students and almost all of the faculty were black or colored. Whites now chose other university settings. Once again, I stood out. Not because of my gender, not because of my age. Because of my color.

I had been invited to attend chapel my first morning in residence. After prayers, we sang hymns with the same beauty of harmonization I knew in Tanzania. During announcements, I was asked to say something of my background and what I hoped to study during my stay. There were smiles of welcome on many faces. Tanzania, women's studies, religious interpretations of exclusion seemed to give us some common ground.

As we left the chapel, several students, men and women, came up to me. When might we meet? They had so many questions. I was overjoyed and looked forward to a continuing engagement with these delightful young people from Namibia, Zimbabwe, Mozambique, and many parts of South Africa. In the late afternoon, when students were in a more leisurely post-class mode, there would be a knock on my door. We'd find chairs on the verandah, a welcome space to talk. The questions didn't stop.

"Tell us about women in the U.S. Do they really think they are liberated?"

"When you have women's seminars in Tanzania, what do they want to learn?"

And I would counter with, "From your experience, in your family, in your country, in your church, what does the rest of the world need to know about you?"

The afternoon sun waned too quickly.

Each morning in chapel, I would sit near the back. In this simple worship space, I could now call several students by name—Anna, Japhet, Moses. As we'd quietly walk outside, greetings were exchanged with encouragement for a new day. We were a community of learners, of believers. This hospitality of spirit was already nourishing me. We are.

And then, a short week later, the United States and Great Britain declared war in Iraq. The announcement came in chapel. The silence roared. A wave of faces slowly turned, looking at me, sitting in the back. There was no nod of recognition; there was no warmth of a smile from anyone. A mass glare, a contemptuous chill swept toward me. Not quite understanding what was happening, it gradually became clear. I represented everything that they were against. Arrogance, domination, superiority, wars. They were not only disdainful of my nationality, they were angry. They all shared war memories.

As we began our usual exit from chapel, no one greeted me, no one shook my hand, everyone did their best to keep their distance. For the next five weeks, every morning in chapel, almost without exception, mention of the Iraq war would cause faces to turn, acknowledging the presence of a pariah. No one would sit by me; no one would share a hymn book. Shunned. They formed a collective stance, a position, an anti-war solidarity. Being seen with me could be interpreted that one was complicit.

The German couple advised me to be very careful. Each day after classes, I would walk out of the university grounds to a shopping area only a few blocks away that had Internet cafes. Their caution was straightforward. "Do not walk beyond that area. You could be mugged and harmed. And it's very likely that no one would come to your aid, especially now."

The weeks crept by. The ostracizing pattern continued. But in the classroom, that was another matter. The reason—Kwame Bediako. Every morning, this slightly built, middle-aged man walked into our "Theology and the African Identity" class carrying his Bible.

Every day, this Ghanaian professor, this widely published scholar greeted us formally in quiet, measured tones. His deep, resonant voice was as startling as the haloed ring of white hair surrounding his very dark face. He never seemed to be in a hurry. He always seemed to be in deep thought, a quizzical expression on his brow.

And then he'd begin. "Ladies and gentlemen, which of you would be so kind as to lead us in prayer? Remember, you may pray in whatever language is your home, your heart language."

Several hands would immediately go up, young men and women from many parts of the continent including the varied sectors of South Africa. The prayer would begin in a language many of us did not know. It didn't matter. We all understood.

Once again, I sat in the back of the class. I didn't want to take time from degree-earning students, so my hand was never up for questioning during class. As for prayer in this august company? I don't think so. One day, we were reading about Jesus's parable when the widow pleads with the judge, over and over again. The discussion became quite lively. And then, Professor Bediako looked right at me and said, "Madam. I am sure you have something to add to this conversation. Please do."

So, I did.

The very last day that I was to audit his class, Professor Bediako walked into class, holding his Bible. He stepped in front of his desk, walked down the aisle towards my chair and asked very gently, "Please, madam, would you pray for us?"

So, I did.

Inside, the classroom was a peaceful haven for learning. Outside, the memories of violence were still erupting. It was a part of everyone's identity, part of their coming of age. Anger, rage, and rebellion may have been quieted and dispelled in the aftermath of dismantling apartheid. Yet, outside, the atmosphere felt like a simmering cauldron.

At the conclusion of one morning's chapel service, not long after the Iraq war declaration, the final hymn was "Onward, Christian Soldiers." When all the verses had been sung, *Amandla! Amandla!* Freedom! Freedom! rang out in an increasing wave of sound. As we walked outside, the chorus became a shouting din, with fists clenched and arms raised. I was ready to return to *sidai, sidai esipa.*

THE

Land   Gender

Reconciliation   Justice

CHALICE

Wonder   Absolutes

Idolatry   Ideology

IS

Innocence   Honor

Ambiguity   Order

A

Stigma   Fidelity

CAULDRON

6 **KITABU** (keeTAHboo)   n. *BOOK*

Books and libraries. I took them for granted. Growing up with their presence, I never questioned their availability, their authority, or their perspectives. Nor did I ever question the why of writing. Discovering how to read the world is a life-long quest.

Aniceti Kitereza ~ John Hope Franklin ~ Gerald Hartwig

Aniceti Kitereza **1968**

There was too much to learn. In 1964, three and a half years after our first arrival at Ilboru Secondary School, we left Tanzania for Indiana University. The world had opened up to us in so many ways that the only solution, it seemed, was a return to the books. For Jerry, a love affair with Africa had been well launched; he would pursue a degree in African History. I would continue with music, which would include the study of ethnomusicology, music in its cultural context.

As a doctoral candidate, Jerry received a Ford Area Foundation grant in 1968 to research the oral history traditions of the Bakerebe, one of three ethnic groups on the island of Ukerewe in Lake Victoria. Ilboru had begun tuning our ears to the East African environment, but living in this new setting as researchers and as parents would require new settings on our learning dial.

Getting to Ukerewe was an adventure. It took two long days traveling by car from Arusha through a part of the Serengeti wilderness that *safari* folk seldom experience. Our kids hardly noticed the rough terrain and continuous jostling. They were too busy looking for giraffe, elephant, lion, and the occasional cheetah. The ferry at Mwanza operated once a day, a precarious-looking barge crammed with people, bicycles, wheelbarrows, and one car, ours. An hour's sail landed us at the port city of Nansio on the shores of Ukerewe. This island, ten miles wide and seventy miles long, home to three distinct ethnic groups, would be our home for nine months.

We brought a trunk full of books as I'd be home schooling Kristopher at fourth grade level, Karl at second, and Kari, a kindergartener. Books. Rare treasures in many parts of the world, including Tanzania. In this setting, oral tradition was still the purveyor of history. Words were committed to memory and told by elders from one generation to another. Book knowledge lived in their minds. Words spoken, not written. Words walked, talked, and sipped tea.

Jerry's task was to interview many *wazee*, elders, whose historical understandings he would then translate to paper and eventually to a book. Little did he know that this research for his own publication would lead to the discovery of an unpublished author on this remote island in Lake Victoria.

Aniceti Kitereza was about seventy-four years old when we first met. He had been identified as one of the important *wazee* with a prodigious historical memory. But he was also known on Ukerewe and in other parts of Tanzania as an ethnographer, a rare collector of folk tales, customs, and proverbs.

When Kitereza was about eight years old, he attended a Catholic mission school. He quickly proved to be an eager and extremely able student. From about 1909 to 1919, he studied under French, German, and Dutch teachers from the Catholic mission. He worked diligently, showing a talent for languages as he mastered Latin, German, French, and Swahili.

Noting his extraordinary abilities, the Catholic priests urged Kitereza to attend the seminary in preparation for the priesthood. But after two years, he left his studies to teach in the same primary school he had attended. Not long after, he married Anna. He chose family and children over celibacy. For a Tanzanian, for an African, your progeny are your legacy, your spirit-life continuation.

Although he was one of the very few educated Kerebe men in his age group, his work opportunities were limited. Because teaching offered so little pay, he sought employment in a government office, but he never rose above the rank of clerk. The attitude of missionaries and colonial administrators at this time barred "natives" from leadership positions. The day had not yet arrived when this attitude would be challenged.

One Catholic father, J. A. Simard, saw what others chose not to notice. He couldn't change Kitereza's employment status, but he could encourage him to write, to chronicle the ways of his people. Kitereza needed little encouragement. He was now old enough to have seen considerable change on Ukerewe and he felt strongly that the earlier traditions of his people should be written. If he didn't preserve this heritage, who would?

The first rendition of Kitereza's book was so academic that Father Simard urged him to write it in story form. By the early fifties, 350 single-spaced typewritten pages had been completed. Upon first reading, Father Simard recognized the value of his work. He asked Kitereza for permission to take a copy with him when he returned home to Quebec with the hope of finding a publisher.

But the priest's untimely death brought that possibility to an end. An American ethnographer visiting Ukerewe in the early sixties had heard about this manuscript. He begged Kitereza for a copy, promising that he would find a publisher. Kitereza never heard from him again. Now there was only one copy left. It was kept under lock and key by the Catholic fathers in Mwanza, a port on the mainland.

During Jerry's initial visits to his home, Kitereza never mentioned his book. And then, about six weeks after we arrived, he told him the story. Jerry listened, returned home, told us and the next day our whole family went to visit him. Sidestepping paddy fields near his home, we started calling out, *Hodi, Hodi*, is anyone home?

We were quickly greeted with *Karibu, Karibu*, welcome, in his deep resonant voice. Clad in a torn red turtleneck sweater and thread-bare khaki pants, Kitereza held on to a walking stick as he slowly made his way to shake our hands. Anna, his wife, brought stools and chairs so we could sit under the canopied mango tree near their mud-and-wattle home. After the fairly extensive greeting process, we came to our reason for coming—his book.

With only one copy left, how would we proceed? Jerry suggested that he would contact the Tanzanian Publishing Company in Dar es Salaam. He would photocopy several pages of the book so that they would be able to determine if it could be published. Within three months, they replied.

Would it be possible to translate it from Kikerebe into Kiswahili? Even though Kitereza's intended audience was the Bakerebe, the people of the island, their language was too limiting. For readership to extend beyond Ukerewe's shores, it must be translated from Kikerebe to Kiswahili.

For Kitereza, this request entailed notebooks, pens, and a laborious page-by-page translation. For the next four months, he worked at a desk fashioned from two orange crates under the mango tree in front of his home. When more paper was needed or ink ran low, we'd bring in new supplies.

When we asked him to tell us about his book, this is what he wrote:

"For fear that these customs, habits and practices of our fathers would die and be forgotten, I began to wonder about this and suddenly I realized that the traditions of this country would be lost for our children and the children yet to be born if they were not written down, for how else will they be preserved? I selected a method: it would be best to put these words in a book. I wrote in *Kikerebe* so that my people could read it.

As I began writing, I searched for those secrets of long ago, things loved and those things despised. I came to realize that the most despised person was one unable to have children whether a man or a woman. It was this understanding that caused me to write about the life of a man and a woman who were unable to have a family, and how they were troubled, worried and anxious. I called the story, *Bwana Myombekere na Bibi Bugonoka*. (Mr. Myombekere and his wife, Mrs. Bugonoka)"

Kitereza's writing goes far beyond the island of Ukerewe. He gave the rest of the world a valuable addition to the accumulating wealth of African ethnography. His writing fights no battles, voices no protest. It is simple, unsophisticated, and objective. It is epic in content and style. His goal was to preserve traditions before they were erased by time. Perhaps Kitereza's endeavors in traditional literature are best understood in his own words: "Words that are spoken, fly in the wind. Words that are written, live forever."

When we left Ukerewe several months later, Jerry hand-carried his dissertation notes. I hand-carried the first hand-written pages of Aniceti's translation from Kikerebe to Kiswahili. The saga of the next thirteen years was a tale of perseverance with publishers, an article in *Natural History*, and innumerable letters between me and Kitereza with one goal: Publish.

In 1981, the Tanzanian Publishing Company's first edition of his book, *Myombokere*, arrived in the post office near Kitereza and Anna's home. By this time, three of the most important people who had eagerly awaited his book in print were no longer living. Anna had died two years before. Jerry had died one year before. Kitereza died just two weeks before his book's arrival.

Two years after the Swahili publication, a German translation was published, heralded with pomp and circumstance at the Goethe Institute in Dar es Salaam. Since then, *Myombekere* has been translated into French and English. His writing was more than a Kerebe chronicle. It was born out of Kitereza and his wife Anna's experience. None of their four children lived beyond the age of four. Childless themselves, how would they be remembered?

Kitereza's book.

JOHN HOPE FRANKLIN   1982

The St. Olaf History Department had invited the prominent historian, John Hope Franklin, to lead a four-day symposium. After many years at the University of Chicago, he had recently accepted the prestigious position as a James B. Duke professor at Duke University. The month was October, the year 1981, almost a year following Jerry's death.

We had never met Dr. Franklin. He arrived at Duke after our departure. We had left Durham and Duke in August of 1980 when Jerry accepted the academic dean's position at St. Olaf. Because of my time and association at Duke, I was invited to join the welcoming group for Dr. Franklin's first morning in Northfield.

When I arrived at the neighborhood Ole Store for this breakfast gathering, several others were already there. As I was introduced, John Hope Franklin unwrapped his long legs from around the counter stool and stood up. He looked down at me from his six-foot-plus stature, saying as he grasped my hand, "Shoonie Hartwig. I am SO glad to meet you. Now I can go home!"

He chuckled and explained, "That's what Ann Scott told me before I left."

As chair of Duke's History Department, Ann had been Jerry's long-term colleague. That Dr. Franklin and I had never met before was not a consideration. Following every event, he would invite me to join his group and include me in the conversation. In this, his gift of remembering, Jerry's spirit was living in my grieving heart. Honoring memory in published works was John Hope's life-long intellectual pursuit. But his understanding of remembering went far beyond his mighty words.

During the course of those few days, John Hope inquired about my family, about my job. When I told him that I had designed a January term course called "The Durham Connection," he probed for details. I explained that it would be an immersion in the black experience. Members of Abiding Savior, our predominantly African American congregation in Durham, North Carolina, had agreed to host students during a month-long stay. Rosa Small, my sister-friend, would co-facilitate with me. Each student would study an aspect of the black experience through interviews and research and write a paper. Scholars at the Universities of North Carolina, Duke, and North Carolina Central would be the primary resources available to the students, as well as community leaders.

"You know," he said, "this is graduate-level inquiry. You tell the administration here that even if you have only two students, you should pilot it. And I will help you. Ann Scott will connect you to my secretary. You let us know when you're coming."

I was stunned and not just a little intimidated. John Hope Franklin. His writings were already legendary in courses focusing on African American history. At that time, *From Slavery to Freedom* was already in its seventh edition and had been translated into multiple languages. A prodigious writer, a Harvard Ph.D. in history and constitutional law, an advisor to United States presidents and Supreme Court judges, he had not only walked in hallowed halls, he had flown in Air Force One.

Only two students signed up for this first offering of The Durham Connection. Not long after writing John Hope to say I was coming, I received a hand-written note from him welcoming me and reminding me to contact his secretary.

Once we arrived in Durham, I made an appointment with some fear and trembling. When I introduced myself to his secretary, her response was, "Well, Shoonie, we wondered when you'd get here. Please come in. John Hope will be here shortly. Unfortunately, he has a meeting this afternoon, but I'm sure something can be arranged."

A few moments later, he strode into his office, wrapped his arms around me in a welcoming embrace, shook hands with each of the women students and said, "I'm so sorry that I don't have time to spend with you right now. But Aurelia, my wife, and I were wondering if you would have time to have dinner with us in our home?"

Somehow, I responded, "We would be delighted." On the appointed evening, John Hope answered the door and ushered us into his lovely home. Aurelia, diminished in size but not in spirit by her husband's stature, welcomed us as warmly as if we were members of their family. The original art work on all of their walls immediately captured our attention. We were given a tour of these significant paintings by Aaron Douglas, Jacob Lawrence, and Henry Ossawa Tanner.

When it was time for dinner, John Hope went into the kitchen to bring out the food, which he announced with some relish would be a menu he not only chose but cooked. Turkey, dressing, sweet potatoes, greens. It was a feast. Before we sat down, he looked at the students and said, "Now, Aurelia will sit at the head of the table, and I will sit opposite her. Shoonie will be next to me on my right and you two can fill in the other seats." Little did I know then that this would become a ritual repeated every January for the next nine years.

After the grand finale of sweet potato pie, while we were still seated at the table, John Hope looked at Gail, one of the two students, and asked, "So, my dear, what is your subject?"

I had no idea what the evening would bring, but I had made sure that both Ellen and Gail were prepared to speak about their research topic and to have questions ready should the opportunity arise. For the next hour, he advised them on faculty resources, community people, books, and articles. As we said our goodbyes and climbed into our rental car, Ellen said, "I've been to the mountain top."

John Hope dedicated his life to remembering with his pen. He wrote about slavery. He wrote about a history that, until his pen and his research recorded it, had not been included in American history. In the graciousness of a wisdom hewn through his own experiences of racism and exclusion, he refused to let life name him or anyone else as lesser than. His greatness was not only in the magnitude of his abilities. His greatness was in his determination to rewrite history. He used his keen intellect to honor the lives of others, not himself. He mentored countless students, colleagues, and friends.

John Hope was well named.

GERALD HARTWIG   1976

In April 2010, I was visiting with Dr. John Shao, the provost of the Lutheran *Tumaini* University in Tanzania. We had been collaborating for ten years on a faculty alliance between colleges of the Evangelical Lutheran Church in America and the several sites of *Tumaini*. Teacher exchanges were providing Tanzanians with reliable Internet accessibility, research materials in libraries, and time to write. Americans were experiencing the realities of higher education in the developing world. They were glimpsing different global perspectives that hopefully would translate to their own classrooms and research.

As we discussed the next year's possibilities, he suddenly asked, "By the way, do you have a picture of your husband?" It was such a switch in the conversation that my surprise must have shown. "I've been thinking," he went on to say, "None of this would have happened if he hadn't brought you here! It would be good to have his picture on our wall."

How true. He did start it all, but not entirely on his own. There were contributing circumstances and people along the way. In December of 1957, Jerry was teaching high school history in Sparta, Wisconsin. I was teaching elementary music in Red Wing, Minnesota. Our wedding was planned for June, but first there were Christmas concerts, so Charlotte boarded a Jefferson bus headed for Red Wing to hear my choirs perform. To my mother's delight, a beloved colleague, Dr. Agnes Larson, was also on the bus.

Charlotte's favorite topics of conversation were her kids and music students. For Dr. Larson, it was her books and history students. Jerry had been a latecomer to the History Department, changing majors annually. Fortunately, Dr. Larson was his advisor. "Where will they be next year?" she asked. "Will they look for teaching positions together?"

"Jerry is thinking about graduate school in guidance and counseling," Charlotte replied. "There is a program at the University of Colorado that he's considering. Shoonie will teach."

Agnes listened, paused a moment and then said, "You know, there's a graduate program at Harvard, a Master of Arts in Teaching. Tell Gerald to come see me when they're in Northfield. This would be good for him. You know, the University of Colorado is all right, but Harvard is better." Little did we know the power of two Olaf women on a Greyhound bus.

If Agnes Larson had had Jerry in class, she would have known him as a good student. Not stellar but solid. Cambridge changed that. Critical thinking thrived in Harvard Square. Actually it crackled and, like the air, was ever present. Even the sidewalks sizzled. It never left him.

51

It followed him to Tanzania where a new focus was finding shape in Jerry's thinking, forging ideas and experience into new possibilities. But there was another ingredient. Passion. He'd fallen in love with Tanzania. He went as a teacher, but he returned as a student, needing to know more about this place and people who captured his head and heart.

In the early 1960s, African studies was emerging as a relatively new graduate course of study in major universities. The civil rights movement and the independence of African states created the impetus for including this long-neglected topic in mainstream curricula.

Jerry, someone whose easy-going stride had walked him rather casually into an Olaf history class, now had a steady purpose in his step. Marriage, Harvard, Tanzania, and soon, four kids sharpened his focus as he began to study East African history at Indiana University in Bloomington.

He soaked up the courses with an insatiable thirst. Not even language requirements daunted him. When he was awarded a Ford Area Fellowship in 1968, we returned to Tanzania and the island of Ukerewe. As he researched the oral traditions of the Bakerebe on this remote island in Lake Victoria, he knew there was a book to be written.

Returning to Bloomington in the fall of 1969 to finish up course requirements, look for a job, and begin writing, his focus was clear. We all noticed. Karl came home from third grade one day and announced, "We had sociology today!"

"Really," I replied. "What did you learn?"

"Well," he said, "we had to draw a picture of our dad at work."

"So, what did you draw?" I asked.

"I drew a picture of him sitting in our cozy chair reading a book with Africa on it! And that's not all," Karl continued. "We had to draw a picture of our dad having fun. You know, it's called recreation."

"And?" I asked.

With a nonchalant tilt of his head, he said, "I drew a picture of him sitting in our cozy chair reading a book with Africa on it."

For Jerry, research and writing were not focused only on a book. He was continuously finding advocacy roles. His first publication in 1974 was a co-edited *Student Africanist's Handbook* that offered references for information on both traditional and contemporary Africa. It was stimulated by the desperation expressed by so many students in their initial attempt to acquaint themselves with the materials available for the study of Africa.

The Art of Survival in East Africa, based on his Ukerewe research, was published in 1976. John Rowe, a colleague from Northwestern University, wrote this: "There has been much talk about little action in terms of meeting a recognized need for social and economic historical studies in Africa. Most work available to scholars and students remains almost entirely politically oriented. Dr. Hartwig was very early in recognizing the need for case studies in social and economic history. He is an imaginative historian who has opened up new areas of inquiry that others might be encouraged to explore."

In 1978, he co-edited *Disease in African History,* a book paving the way for inclusion of disease and medicine in historical research. Of course, he also published innumerable journal articles that demonstrated his inter-disciplinary approach. In 1978, he edited a collection of books for younger readers called *African Sketches*. Whether he was advocating that oral traditions be included in research paradigms or providing African resources for scholars new to the field or African contextual reading material for high school students, Jerry's heart and mind were one.

THE SCRIM

Diffuses shadow
    And form

              Color and shade

Threads image
    And pattern

              Darkness and light

Weaves sight
    And sound

              Disperses and ignites

Signifies possibility
    And definition

              Eludes and reveals

Fuses voice
    And lens

              Focus and pattern .

Filtering
    Perception
        Interpretation
            Prescription
                Assumption

Strobes explode
    Transposing
        Scrim
           and
              Script

7 **UHUSIANO** (oohooseeAHNoh)   n. *PARTNERSHIP,*
RELATIONSHIP

The varieties are as numerous as are the modes of engagement as are the whys behind our motivations for going to that other place. The spiritual "Wade in the water, children, God's gonna' trouble the water" grew out of slave experiences. Wading is slow going. The call and response of spirituals deepens an awareness of how a common goal through troubled waters can bring us to the point where we're singing together. Whether we are facilitating or participating in organizational partnerships, the structure of each determines our role. And that leads us to a continuous discovery process in our receiving and in our giving, as a host or as a guest. Relationships, off the page, inevitably draw us into troubled waters.

Lutheran College Consortium Tanzania ~ Mwangaza ~ Guest/Host

LUTHERAN COLLEGE CONSORTIUM TANZANIA 1985

Nineteen eighty was a difficult year marked by continued family tragedies. In August, we moved from North Carolina back to Minnesota, back to the norms of where I grew up, where Lutherans, Scandinavians, and white worldviews predominated. We had returned to Northfield, Minnesota, where I was raised, and to the college where Jerry and I met. We were again in a white majority environment where Jerry would be the academic dean at St. Olaf College. We hoped that his years of enculturation in other settings would make him an effective advocate for global learning. We never found out. Jerry died from a massive heart attack six weeks later.

Jerry and I had planned a return trip to Tanzania before he took the position at St. Olaf. We wanted our older kids to see this part of our world again as young adults and to take our youngest for his first visit. I honored that plan but with an additional goal. I would begin my part-time work at St. Olaf in the fall. I hoped to make connections at the University of Dar es Salaam. But it had been twenty years since I'd been in Tanzania. A lot had changed.

In Tanzania, the eighties were difficult years. *Ujamaa*, Julius Nyerere's promulgation of socialist interdependence was faltering. Economically, the costs of becoming self-sustaining as a fledgling independent country were fraying the already meager holdings of subsistence farmers. Shopping for the basics of soap, sugar, and tea was an exercise in futility.

The sense of responsibility to one's neighbors, however, did not falter. President Nyerere supported Ugandan forces in ousting Idi Amin at a cost that the country could ill afford. Similarly, Tanzania became a harboring place for many fleeing South Africa, Mozambique, and Botswana during the years of apartheid struggles.

And what of education? In those sparse economic times with political ferment roiling outside Tanzania's borders, the University of Dar es Salaam was as young as the country, a mere twenty years old. Many professors sought employment in other parts of the world because salaries in Tanzania were not dependable. The brain drain on the country was significant. Fortunately, there were those whose choices were limited and others who were determined to stay. The university stumbled its way through the decade.

This was the educational environment I entered that July. Introductions had preceded me. Dave Simonson, who worked with the Maasai in the Arusha region, knew the right connection. His name was Justin Maeda, a teacher at the university and a Lutheran. He was the son of Joel Maeda, who directed the Education Department in the newly emerging Evangelical Lutheran Church in Tanzania. Justin shared his family's heritage of education, faith, and commitment to country.

Educated in the United States, Justin had returned to head Development Studies at the University of Dar es Salaam. However, President Julius Nyerere invited him to leave the university and assist him in the government. This change in Justin's work assignment turned out to be significant. He no longer resided in a cramped office at the university. In his new post, he had a spacious room in the White House, a magisterial government building on Haillie Selassie Road in Dar es Salaam.

When a time for our meeting was determined, Justin informed me that transportation would be arranged. A car would be sent to the hotel where I was staying. A car, indeed. My jaw dropped when a white Peugot pulled up, singularly adorned with the Tanzanian flag indicating its owner: the President's Office.

The parting of the Red Sea was reenacted as we slowly made our way to the White House. People on foot and others behind various wheeled vehicles suddenly moved to the side of the road with wild shouts and exultant hand waving.

The entrance to the White House was as grand as the Tanzanian flag was magical. Two life-size taxidermied lions guarded the doorway. The message was clear. Power resides here. I was ushered into a formal, sunny conference room where Justin welcomed me. If first blinks were any indication of how business would be handled, it was going to be brisk and straightforward. With hardly any prelude, Justin looked at me and asked in a very direct, almost stern tone, "Where have you been?"

He was seated at the table, a man of medium build, wearing the Tanzanian Mao suit, as crisp in attire as he would be for an interrogation. He had earned his doctorate in Germany by the time he was in his early thirties. Fluent in at least five languages, an academic presenter at United Nations Development Program meetings, a speaker at many international gatherings on development issues from a Tanzanian perspective, Justin was a man with a mission. Into that impressive and humbling milieu, I was welcomed.

His rather abrupt question to me was not one that I had imagined. Yet in the years following that hour of planning and conjecturing, I have often reflected on its import and significance. As an emerging independent country, Tanzania's embrace of *ujamaa* for self-sufficiency was floundering. Yet its intention to build an educated public never waned. President Nyerere had inaugurated the Universal Primary Education plan to assure a foundation of literacy for all Tanzanian citizens.

In 1981, however, the percentage of teenagers in secondary schools throughout Tanzania, to say nothing of those trained at the University of Dar es Salaam, was in the low single digits. Nyerere's socialism embraced a grassroots philosophy reflected in his focus on primary school accessibility for all citizens. Secondary and higher education suffered from budget shortfalls.

How does a newly independent country govern, teach, heal, and legislate when training opportunities for its youth are so limited? During the 1980s, scholarships were offered by developed nations to Tanzania and other countries in the developing world. More was at stake than education degrees. By offering this form of international aid, powerful countries could shape ideologies as well as form future alliances. The Soviet Union led the way in education scholarships. The United States had offered little. For countries like Tanzania, educational choices were limited.

During that first conversation with Justin, the Lutheran College Consortium (LCCT) for Tanzania found a birthing place. At its center would be several basic guidelines. It would be an exchange of American and Tanzanian participants. The basic premise of LCCT: learning opportunities would be made available for students in both countries to enhance their worldview and skill development.

When I returned to St. Olaf, I initiated conversations that would continue for four years between provosts at the University of Dar es Salaam and the academic deans of several Lutheran colleges. Once again, I was entering new territory. There were very few opportunities for students from the United States to study in sub-Saharan Africa, and most existing programs did not include an exchange component. Thanks to LCCT, not only would our students have an international learning experience, so would Tanzanians.

The American students would matriculate at the University of Dar es Salaam like any other student, live in the dormitory, eat in the cafeteria, and attend classes with everyone else. They would be completely integrated into university life. A faculty member would accompany them from the United States and stay in Dar es Salaam for a two-week orientation period. After that, the students would be responsible to the university authorities. Tanzanian students would follow a similar pattern in this country.

Presidents of five Lutheran colleges and their academic deans were the first to sign on. But then a faculty representative needed to be identified on each college campus, one who would champion this program and encourage student participation. This was no easy task. At the time, curricula in our Lutheran colleges had little representation of the developing world. In addition, there were few study-abroad programs within the African continent. We were breaking new ground.

Suddenly, two years into the planning, the University of Dar es Salaam indicated that they would send only faculty, those teachers who needed time to research their doctoral literature review, rather than students. This decision was more than a curve ball. We came close to striking out. Financial considerations were significant in our deliberations. Faculty would not stay in a dormitory with students. They would expect different accommodations. Housing costs could bring our years of negotiation to a halt. Yet the conversations continued.

For four years, we drank a lot of tea; we made a lot of phone calls; we wrote and revised many memos of understanding. In 1985, I accompanied the first four students to the University of Dar es Salaam. It was memorable. For starters, none of the students had ever traveled outside the United States. Conditions at the university were challenging. There was no running water. Truckloads of water containers were driven in daily. The library holdings were, generally speaking, minimal and out of date. Nonetheless, everyone persevered.

Throughout the developing world, access to computer technology and library resources continues to be problematic, unreliable, and in many areas inaccessible. It is not enough to provide American students with an international or intercultural experience. Reciprocity for students and faculty is as important for Tanzanians as it is for Americans. Reciprocal alliances bring everyone to the same table. This is where all student participants learn life needs, life histories, and life ways. This is where all faculty participants learn new content enlightened through experience and research. Students and faculty steeped in this learning will have earned a degree for which there is not yet a major. There should be.

For thirty-three years, the Lutheran College Consortium for Tanzania was the partnership model at the University of Dar es Salaam for all of their student exchange programs - reciprocity between the two countries - the cornerstone of LCCT.

MWANGAZA 1996

Mwangaza. As a word in Swahili, it means enlightenment. As an organization, it describes a grassroots, faith-based partnership linking participants from twenty dioceses of the Evangelical Lutheran Church in Tanzania with twenty synods of the Evangelical Lutheran Church in the United States in leadership development. Mwangaza Education for Partnership ELCT/ELCA has been our title since we began in 1996. What we could see then and what we see now continues to evolve. We couldn't have imagined how this organic structure would grow in program, in implementation, and in relationships. Nor could I have imagined my role within Mwangaza.

It all started in the early years of the Lutheran College Consortium for Tanzania program. I accompanied students to the university each July, staying for the two weeks of orientation. However, in 1988, I received an invitation from two Tanzanian Lutheran bishops to visit their secondary schools. This meant I'd extend my time in Tanzania for several more weeks. I had been working for years at the university level. Now, I was asked to begin observing secondary education. The bishops had good reason to be concerned.

Soon after independence in 1961, Tanganyika (which would merge with Zanzibar and become Tanzania in 1964) nationalized most of its secondary schools. Twenty-five years later, that decision was reversed. The government acknowledged its inability to adequately support secondary schools. Non-government organizations were invited to support education as they had in the past. The Evangelical Lutheran Church in Tanzania agreed.

It was into this milieu that I was invited as an educator who had a history in the country. For several weeks each year, I would visit schools and listen to teachers talk about their particular setting, their needs as teachers, and the challenges for their students. The primary question I'd ask was: "What do you need to make a difference?"

It was a first. No one was asking this question. They couldn't afford to. It's hard to dream when you're hungry. It's hard to imagine when your life soil is caked and dry. Yet these teachers dared to name what could make a difference in their teaching, in their schools. There is empowerment in this process for there is ownership in naming what needs to be learned. There is danger in this process for it threatens the status quo.

By 1994, my school visits had expanded from two dioceses, or regions, to five at the request of the national Lutheran Church in Tanzania. That same year in July, I met with representative teachers from each diocese to imagine our way forward together. It was at that meeting that we named ourselves. There are many words to describe light in Swahili. *Mwangaza*, however, is more than illumination for your path. It is what the path reveals back to you, a process of enlightenment.

We also named answers to the question "What do you need that would make a difference?" Teachers cited these primary needs: English-language proficiency, subject content, methodologies, and material resources. Now we had the "what" in the needs quotient. The "how" was directed to me.

After eight years of informal listening and learning with secondary school teachers, I was invited by the Evangelical Lutheran Church in Tanzania to be the director of this fledgling organization called Mwangaza and to facilitate the process of developing educational partnerships. At this time, the Evangelical Lutheran Church in America had designed a companion program linking all of their synods to international church bodies. An organizational structure was in place.

Before moving to Tanzania in 1996, I resigned from St. Olaf College. I had sold my house and put selected belongings in long-term storage. In the beginning, I was the only employee, but we were already connected to many teachers through our first exchange between five ELCT dioceses and five ELCA synods.

Within our first year, a foundation was built. It started with teachers in Tanzania spending two months in their companion region in the states. For example, a math, science, or English teacher from Iringa went to St. Paul, Minnesota. A teacher from Dar es Salaam went to Upper Peninsula, Michigan. Each Tanzanian teacher was paired with a United States teacher. Together, they developed lesson plans on difficult topics in the syllabus. The following June, the U.S. teachers traveled to their companion regions in Tanzania, and as a team, each pair led seminars for teachers throughout that diocese. It worked well.

Collaboration in learning and in teaching is possible when there is commonality in purpose. Education provided that base. Within four years, all twenty dioceses of the ELCT requested partnership with Mwangaza, which made us national in scope. It also made us complicated in organizational structure. The norm is bilateral engagements between two partners, not shared ownership among twenty. Keeping our common goal in front of us was an ongoing challenge.

In 1998, I attended a Mwangaza seminar in the southern part of Tanzania. The teachers from that region, along with their headmaster, had asked to meet with me to talk about the challenges they were facing. Haran, the newly appointed headmaster, explained that he had selected two teachers to go into neighboring areas to talk with parents and encourage them to send their children to this new school.

But when the teacher spoke with Maasai herdsmen, they asked him, "If we send our children to you, will they come home to take care of us once they have finished school?"

And when the teacher went to the Ruaha fisherman, they said, "If our children stay home, they will learn how to fish, how to live. What will you teach them?"

Then Haran looked at me and said, "Mama, what should we tell them?"

I had no ready answer. Of course, I gave them the canned versions of why we educate, but all the while I knew it wasn't getting to the heart of the matter. Not here where sustaining life is a daily concern, where skills for survival are understood to be based in land, cattle, and ritual.

The next day, I was at the university in Iringa to meet with the vice provost. The headmaster's question was uppermost in my mind. After telling the story, I asked, "What would you say?" Without any hesitation, the vice provost replied, "We have to learn how to care for one another, with hope."

We continue to translate that understanding into relevant programs. Within a year of this conversation, we were asked by several Tanzanian teachers, "What can Mwangaza do about educating our girls? Do you know that fifty percent of them don't complete secondary school?"

After conferring with a team of women leaders, we designed a new program for women and their daughters that we called *Binti-Mama* or Daughters-Mothers. Taught in Kiswahili, this intergenerational seminar provided information on nutrition, women's health, gender awareness, and children's rights.

Within a short time, we were asked by women first, and later men, "What can Mwangaza do about educating our young people and our community members about HIV/AIDS?" After conferring with a team of community leaders, we designed a new program that included information about this virus but also about attitudes and behaviors needed for change in gender relationships.

When I first read Paolo Friere's *Pedagogy of the Oppressed* in the early 1970s, I had no idea that I would be facilitating an adaptation of his theories through Mwangaza. Friere's basic premise is that until we can name what we need to learn, until we learn it in dialogue, until we question, only then will we be empowered to teach others what we have learned. Only then will education be rooted in a relevant context of living it.

But living Mwangaza's education is revolutionary. Teachers are learning to let go of their didactic, authoritarian methods in classrooms. They are challenged to change personal relationships with students that too often are harassing and sexually inappropriate. Administrators are encouraged to develop accountability structures that nurture a safe, disciplined learning environment. These are radical changes in power structures built on historical cultural and gender-based privilege that dictates "who can" and "who can't" with impunity.

Mwangaza'a Community Health and *Binti-Mama* programs address many issues that are culturally sensitive and others that are bound in tradition. Assumed gender roles in work, school, home, and church may seem benign. Unpack them, however, and rape, incest, beatings, female genital mutilation, malnutrition, and exploitation of the girl child leap out.

In our present *Binti-Mama* program, the indicators that change is needed include early pregnancies, beating, rape, and girls' inability to complete secondary school. One woman looked at our plan, shook her head and said, "Tanzanian women are SHY!! It's a challenge just to teach them about the cause and effect of these topics. But change? WHERE ARE THE BOYS AND MEN? When will the girls and women you train be empowered to learn and then advocate for change with the men?" It's a Herculean challenge.

Consequently, we are engaged in a multi-year process to train individual Tanzanian teams to bring about critically needed cultural change. Our role is to provide information they request on various topics, methods, and advocacy. Our goal is to develop a model for intervention based on indicators of change which will demonstrate the effectiveness of this process.

We have initiated an innovative literacy approach to support the learning process. Mwangaza is creating its own mini-books, using an eight-by-eleven-inch sheet of paper folded twice. They are written in English or Kiswahili, depending on our audience. Each book contains relevant information about a subject such as the digestive system, health hazards from unsafe drinking water, or teen pregnancy. The power of printed material, the power of illustrations and diagrams, the power of owning your own book, lies within a twice-folded piece of paper.

Following a seminar in community health, Zacharia, holding one of his mini-books, said, "Until I came here to Mwangaza, my brain was asleep. It is now awake!"

Student responses in evaluations say, "These books help me understand English so much better, and the stories I like because they are about us."

Following a seminar for intergenerational women, a participant holding the seven mini-books prepared for the course asked, "Please, do we have to give these books back?" The staff, surprised by the question, replied, "But of course these are yours. They are yours to use at home and they are yours to use when you train other women in your dioceses." The women broke out in exultant trills.

Not only have our programs evolved, our administrative structure has also changed. Since I retired as director in 2003, I continue as consultant. The professional staff at Mwangaza is all Tanzanian; the Mwangaza board of regional representatives provides guidance and accountability. Friends of Mwangaza, the United States-based support organization, seeks financial support and volunteers for Mwangaza's outreach. Decision-making is shared.

Education as the welcoming table for change is powerful in that no one is without credentials. We have all been learners; there are many ways to play a role. The challenge is finding the place where we best contribute without taking up too much space, always leaving room for others at the table. It is this mutuality that forges common purpose, where contributions in skill, knowledge, and support come from both hemispheres. This is our sustainability, calling one another by name.

There is a deep, gnawing hunger in the world. Hunger for food, hunger for justice, hunger for knowledge, hunger for choice. Through Mwangaza, we are learning how to read the world together with imagination and hope. It is an inexpressible privilege.

We are.

Hidden within each of the following paragraphs are perceptions of the myriad ways we may be seen or how we see others. Think of them as if you were taking an eye examination. It is the smallest font that requires the strongest lenses.

Two Tanzanian teachers were in the United States as part of our Mwangaza exchange. Their host family brought them to an Adult Forum in their church to hear about new farming initiatives. When the presenters reported that a cow's milk production was increased significantly if mattresses were available rather than a cold cement floor, four startled eyes looked at me. "*Wamesema godoro? Kweli? N'gombe wanatumia GODOROS?* Did they say mattresses? Really? The cows are using MATTRESSES?"

Several days after arriving at the University of Dar es Salaam with a group of LCCT college students, there was a loud pounding on my door. One young woman strode into my room, stood in front of me with hands on her hips declaring indignantly, "You know, this place, well, almost EVERYONE is black, and they hardly ever speak English!"

A Tanzanian pastor was preparing several church members who would be welcoming Americans into their homes. "The first thing they'll ask is if you have Internet. The second thing they'll ask is if you have a place to charge their phone and camera."

A Tanzanian friend with years of international experience who was a published scholar and a church education leader had just returned from a board meeting that concerned the development of a university in Tanzania. Those attending included several Americans. My friend looked at me and said somewhat wearily, "You know, it is a testament to the Gospel that we continue to believe in spite of many missionaries."

If you change one vowel in any Kiswahili word, you could be in trouble. One student teacher volunteer was working hard on her language skills. Every week, she would go to the local *duka*, or shop, and say, "*Naomba chupi cha maji.*" She thought she was asking for a bottle of water. However, *chupi* is underpants and *chupa* is bottle. The shopkeeper never said a thing.

Encouraged to bring pictures of her family, one volunteer at Mwangaza had many photos of her dogs which she proudly showed our staff. "These are my babies," she said. In amazement and disbelief, one teacher looked to me and said, "*Watoto wake ni mbwa*? Her dogs are her family?"

An LCCT student and I were walking across the University of Dar es Salaam campus. As we passed several young men holding hands, a very puzzled Peter asked, "What is that all about?"

It was a beautiful March morning in southern Minnesota. Jacob, a recently arrived Tanzanian teacher, looked outside. Seeing the brilliant sun, he opened the door and walked to the sidewalk. After a few minutes, he was very, very cold; his short-sleeved shirt was not sufficient. Trying to get back in the house, he discovered the door had locked. His host had left early in the morning and wouldn't return for several hours. Shivering, Jacob knocked on four doors before anyone invited him in out of the cold.

One of our LCCT students, a Sissy Spacek look-alike with long blond hair and small stature, tired of persistent attention from male students. After repeated advances, she deftly decked one young man. Her yellow belt in karate was as effective as the bush telegraph which said, "When she says no, she means no!"

Upon her return from two years as a volunteer teacher in Tanzania, Laura was delighted to meet a family friend and tell her just a bit of her experiences. Almost immediately, her friend interrupted her to say, "How exciting it must have been for you. But tell me, I know of another volunteer in Ghana. Perhaps you've met?"

"This is our library!" said a teacher as she proudly opened the door to a room with more space on the shelves than books. At random, I picked out one. *Mental Health Issues in Sweden*. Another, *The Mississippi River*. "Tell me," I asked, "do students read many of these books?" "Well, not really," she said with a shrug of her shoulders.

Loshoro. In Maasai communities, it is the favored beverage. The basic ingredients are clabbered milk and corn. Wrapped in a *khanga*, as is the custom for women attending an *msiba*, the condolence gathering prior to a funeral, I'd hoped to greet the widow and exit fairly quickly. However, I was ushered inside a makeshift tent and asked to sit between the widow and her sister-in-law. When a very large cup of *loshoro* was offered me, I looked at it with dismay. Even the very smallest sips didn't decrease the remaining amount. Repeated offers to fill up my cup brought a quick reply, "*Nimeshiba kabisa, asante!* I am well satisfied, thank you." An endless, bottomless cup.

It had been a long, hot, dusty trip over potholed roads. Finally arriving at the Singida guest house in northwest Tanzania, I wearily went to the common shower room. My body felt like every pore was filled with red silt. I eagerly turned on the tap, but nothing happened. I waited and tried again with the same result. Hearing a soft knock on the door, I opened it to see a young woman holding a quart sized can, half full of *maji*, water. "*Karibu*," she said, offering me this precious gift.

A teacher volunteer, eagerly awaiting his parents' visit, exclaimed: "Actually, you know, I'm really surprised they're coming HERE. When my sister went to France, of course they went there. But Tanzania? What's here?" And he walked off with a dismissive shrug of his shoulders.

During my years at St. Olaf, I taught a class on American Racial Multicultural Studies. We were discussing the civil rights movement. One student, directing his question to the only African American in class, asked, "What do you people think about non-violence?"

A free prescription: Consider a daily cocktail of a listening ear, a respectful mind, and a compassionate heart with generous splashes of humor and gratitude.

TEMPTATION

It's a grave temptation to want to help people

Dorothy Day said so

I don't understand

The marginalized
The forgotten
The have-nots

They   need   help!

I have ideas
I have solutions
I have money
I have clothes
I have books
I have ideas
I have talents
I can help!

Temptation?

What's the problem?

Who is Jesus anyway?

8 **WANAWAKE NA WATOTO** (WahnahWAHkaye nah WahTOHtoh)
pro. *WOMEN AND CHILDREN*

"If the first woman God ever made was strong enough to turn the world upside down all alone, women together ought to be able to turn it back and get it right side up again." Sojourner Truth's words are ageless. But to live them requires courage, bravery, and resiliency of women world-wide. If you listen, you will hear a women's chorus singing, singing for themselves and for their children.

Flore ~ Mzungu ~ Gloria C

FLORE 2003

When we initiated our *Binti-Mama* program in 1998, a team of women determined that the first topics should include nutrition, women's life cycle, women's health, and advocacy for girls' education. But in 2000, there was a new vocabulary word in Kiswahili, *UKIMWI*, for HIV/AIDS. Teenage girls were already at high risk to not complete secondary education. Now *UKIMWI* added a desperate and urgent reality to their and their mothers' lives. However, due to the pervasive stigma of this disease, it was hidden, seldom acknowledged. It was faceless.

At the request of pastors from several regions in Tanzania, Mwangaza offered a special seminar addressing marriage, stewardship, and HIV/AIDS. A social worker in Arusha agreed to teach the section on *UKIMWI* and asked if she could bring a young mother living with AIDS to tell her story. When Flore walked into the gathering of some thirty men, she sat quietly on a chair at the front of the room. Her lovely tie-dyed gown hid her wraithlike figure. The quiet in the room was deafening as she began her story.

70

"I have been married for fifteen years," she began. "My husband and I have three children. For years, I have known that my husband has been with other women. He travels for his work and so he is gone from home sometimes weeks at a time. I never said anything. As his wife, it was not my place. But then that changed with *UKIMWI*. And I was afraid. So when my husband demanded that I would be his wife, I refused."

At this point, a collective intake of breath was audible. Such behavior. Unthinkable.

But Flore continued. "Each time I refused, my husband would beat me. Finally, I went home, as is our custom, and I told my parents. They said: 'Go home, forgive him, it is your duty, be patient.'

"And so I returned, but my husband's behavior didn't change. Again, he'd beat me. And then I went to the village elders, as is our custom. They said: 'Go home, forgive him, it is your duty, be patient.'

"But the beatings continued. Finally, I went to my pastor, as is our custom, and he said: 'Go home, forgive him, it is your duty, be patient.'"

There was a stillness in the room filled with emotions of sorrow, anxiety, and perhaps fear. After a few minutes, one pastor stood, and he said, "*Tusamehe*. Forgive us."

Indeed there is much in this world to forgive for behaviors that insist on male dominance at any cost. There are millions of women like Flore who are waiting patiently to die throughout Tanzania and elsewhere in the world. World-wide, there are customs, there are laws, there are scriptural interpretations that insist on male superiority and deny women and children lives free from fear, violence, and disenfranchisement.

There are many aspects of life in Tanzania that cause sensory overload. The rawness of poverty is in your face; it is in your nostrils. In the midst of barrenness, however, is the eruption of women's laughter, women's indomitable courage, women's unshakeable faith. It's a force to be reckoned with, a resilient life-knowing to be celebrated and lived to the fullest. This is Flore.

She is not waiting patiently, to die.

SERVING SLAVERY

They are the ones
    All shapes sizes turbaned cloaked shaved nappy

        Chadors shorts dior khanga
            Elegance salon-shaped barefoot pierced
            Hues hewn in birthing

They are the ones
    Mutilated for pleasure
        Starved for beauty
            Ostracized for choices
                Voiced for obeisance

They are the ones
    Mothers daughters wives sisters friends
    Bound
        Feet
        Brain
        Will
        Potential

        servingservingservingserving

    We are the ones   We are the ones

        We are the ones
        Who make it

        So

Who am I? It never seemed to be a difficult question. Depending on the setting, my answer could be relatively straightforward. When I was at Duke, I was Jerry's wife. When I was teaching music at North Carolina Central University, I was Ms. Hartwig. When I was at a school event, I was my kids' mom. Identity in name and what it means in its fullest context changes over the years. It changes with job, settings, relationships, responsibilities, and circumstances.

During the seven years I lived in Tanzania as director with Mwangaza, I was named differently. Some were relatively easy. When I was introduced in an educational or church setting, it would always start with, "Dr. Shoonie." This was a significant acknowledgement that I was a woman with a doctorate. I was a woman with credentials that were important to our colleagues in the formal sector. But it didn't last long. First and foremost, I was Mama Shoonie.

My identity as a mama was far superior to doctor. Within much of Africa, bearing children demonstrates a woman's capacity-building ability. Without children, as a woman, you are simply unfulfilled. Although I was *mjane*, a widow, this name was never used. The term widow, by the way, means without. In Tanzanian society, widowed women are desperately without, disinherited at every level. Fortunately, it was a name that didn't apply to me in their setting.

But *mzungu*, that identity marker was significant. Literally it means one who walks in circles and is addressed to any expatriate irrespective of ethnicity. Over the last several decades, it has evolved to be a derogatory term. We bear an historical burden of oppression and with it all the negative stereotypes. However, it also names us as potential donors for everything from school fees to food for a day. In addition to being a potentially bottomless financial resource, we are also presumed to be knowledgeable on all subjects. The questions, the concerns, the requests are as unexpected as they are daunting.

It wasn't even seven a.m. when I heard a *hodi* at my door. "Is anyone home?" It was too early, said my body. "What now?" said my irritated heart as I responded, *karibu*. When I opened the door, there were five women assembled on the verandah, already seated in the wooden chairs, greeting me with expectant faces.

Swaddled in the arms of one mama lay the still form of her infant daughter. As she talked, she unfolded the blanket and revealed a hydrocephalic child. Stunned to speechlessness, I could barely take in her words as I looked in disbelief at a form I'd only seen in pictures. The head was at least twice its normal size. The eyes were mere slits, the nose flattened, the mouth a bird's opening. The forehead sloped to a skull so elongated that my eyes could not sense its human form. Yet there was no doubt that this was a precious child whose mama was desperate.

Looking up at me, she said, "Mama, my child, she is so quiet. She won't nurse; she won't eat. She doesn't even cry! I have taken her to the hospital and they tell me there is nothing to be done. But, mama, this is my baby. What can I do?"

As we talked, it was clear that they had tried every possibility in seeking help for this child. They had been to the hospital. Not just one but several. They had heard the responses of the nurses. They had returned because certainly what they heard the first time wasn't true. Now they came to me. Surely, surely this mama, this *mzungu*, would tell them what to do. Surely, she would have an answer. She would know how to bring life to this swaddled, this much too quiet baby.

I didn't have an answer. But I knew more than they would ever want to know. I knew the heart-rending wail that would soon be theirs. The keening for a child no longer living has no name, no translation; it is beyond speech. It is sorrow so deep and eviscerating, it is beyond vocabulary. There is no identity word for a mama whose child dies. It is too awful to name.

Yet, I also knew that whenever that mama was asked, "How many children do you have?" that her answer would always include this little one. Her identity as a mama would never, ever deny the spirit living of this child. It is not so in our culture where death is denied, loss is an aberration. Living amidst this knowing of life-death realities has been a life-giving gift.

GLORIA C 1978

We met under extraordinary circumstances. It was in 1978, a Sunday afternoon following church at Abiding Savior in Durham when I answered the phone. A friend from church said, "I know this is going to be very unusual, but I have a request. You see, my sister Gloria's son committed suicide in her living room last week. She, along with two of her other children, witnessed it. I've heard that you and Jerry attend some kind of meetings with other parents whose children have died. Do you suppose you could take Gloria with you some time?"

Almost stunned to speechlessness, I said, "Barbara, of course we could do this, but do you really think she would want to go? We meet in Chapel Hill and everyone is white. We've never met Gloria and she has to be reeling with grief."

"I've already told her about you and she really wants to meet you," she replied.

Several weeks later we picked her up at her apartment in a public housing complex. From the first meeting, Jerry and I were struck with Gloria's profound human understanding. Among the several university and professional people in our Compassionate Friends group, she was the one who could most clearly articulate the turbulent emotions we were all experiencing. After she'd attended several meetings, she said, "It is so sad when mens can't cry."

About a year later, as we drove Gloria home, I told her that we wouldn't be going to the next meeting because our church was having a retreat in the mountains. "A retreat?" she asked. "What does that mean?" I explained a bit and she shook her head. "I've never heard of anything like that. Retreat." A new word.

Sometime later, I was talking with sister-friend Rosa and told her about Gloria. Rosa responded, "We should have a women's retreat. We could have several women from church and Gloria could bring her friends." It happened. Gloria invited five friends, all of whom worked with her at Duke University Hospital. Gloria was an elevator operator, and the others were employed in the laundry or kitchen.

We arrived at Luther Rock late in the afternoon armed with fried chicken, biscuits, greens, and pies for starters. The Duke group disappeared after a walkabout. No kids, no responsibilities? Time for a nap. When we gathered to eat and begin that getting-to-know-you process, not one woman in Gloria's group had ever had time out like this. Four of them were single parents; all of them had several dependent children as well as extended family members for whom they bore primary responsible.

Linda, a social worker from church, suggested we try an exercise that she'd often used. She gave each of us a piece of paper. The instructions seemed straightforward. "Draw a circle like a pie," she said. "Now divide it into eight wedges. Think about each piece of the pie as ten years of your life. In each one, write down what you did, what you liked to do, what you wanted to do, the important people in your life. When you get to whatever is your present decade, write what you want to do in the future."

When we started going around the circle, describing each decade, I began to stand out. Significantly. Not only was I the only white woman present, I was the only one who repeatedly, decade after decade, spoke of creativity, whether singing, playing the piano or flute, reading, or traveling.

The wedge that caused us to really get down was the final one. What did we want to do in the future, and with whom? Where did we want to go? It was my turn. I had simply written, "I want to grow old with my husband." There was this eerie quiet. No one said a word. Then one of Gloria's friends asked, "When can we meet him?!" and we all broke up in laughter.

When they did meet him, it was a bit of a love feast. Jerry, no surprise, was rather delighted to be included but at first admitted to being a tad intimidated. It didn't last long.

One of Gloria's sisters was the secretary in Duke's History Department. After our move from Durham to Northfield, after Jerry's death, I had a phone call from her. "Shoonie," she said, "We have an early Christmas present for you. Would it be convenient if we sent Gloria to spend a weekend with you and your kids, say, in early December?"

Gloria had never been in a plane. Nor had she traveled outside of North Carolina. One friend lent her an ankle-length seal coat; another, heavy boots. Meeting her at the Minneapolis airport was to welcome a woolly mammoth. I couldn't tell you what we talked about. I couldn't tell you where we went. I don't remember. But this is as clear to me now as it was thirty-four years ago. Gloria's presence midst me and my grieving children was a balm in Gilead. She was a History Department gift beyond imagining.

Gloria arrived the weekend of St. Olaf's Christmas concert.

She used Jerry's ticket.

9 KWA NINI? (kwahNEEnee)   adv. *WHY?*

Why do we cross over? What are our motivating factors? Our answers make all the difference.

DURHAM, NORTH CAROLINA 1970

No one had asked us "why?" until we moved to Durham, North Carolina, in 1970. A year after returning from our research on Ukerewe, we finished our degrees at Indiana University and headed to Duke University where Jerry would teach African history. Once again, we were in new territory—Ivy League in the South, magnolias, sweet potato pie, basketball, and "How y'all doin'?"

Not long after we joined Abiding Savior Lutheran Church, Roamless Hudson came up to me and said, "So, Shoonie, when are you going to write your book?" I remember my astonishment and then maybe, I hope, some laughter as I replied, "When you co-author with me." I was completely unprepared for that question or the hidden meaning in it.

Durham's civil rights participation was very alive in this congregation. Roamless taught at St. Augustine College in Raleigh. He had been an integral part of the civil rights movement as had the majority of the church membership. They marched; they joined coalitions; they formed new alliances. And it wasn't over.

About a year later, we were invited to an afternoon gathering of church members at the home of good friends, Roland and Gloria Cardwell. We were there to meet a visiting Lutheran from Ohio. He was one of a few black representatives on the Ohio Lutheran Synod Council. Initially, the conversation was casual as we talked about church and national politics.

Then Arne looked at Jerry and me and said, "Now tell me, why is it you're messin' around with these black folk?" Since we were the only white folk in this gathering, the question was for us, only.

Bill Small, a professor at the University of North Carolina, shot to his feet, and said somewhat protectively, "Now look here..."

Gloria interrupted with "Hey!" from the chaise lounge where she sat. Casually crossing her long legs, she leaned back, looked at everyone, and said, "Let them talk. They can take care of themselves." All eyes were on us.

Jerry started, somewhat nervously at first, but his voice gained strength. "If we hadn't gone to Tanzania, we probably wouldn't be here. What we learned there about bright students with so few options, about an educational system that denied them their heritage was completely beyond our experience. And then we went to the island of Ukerewe, and I was at the feet of elders whose knowledge in memory would take years to assemble. The richness of music traditions and the wit and wisdom of folklore captured our imagination.

"Since moving here," he continued, "with Kris and Karl in middle school, we've been appalled at the lack of information in their studies about Africa and the African American experience. Western worldview prevails. But here at Abiding Savior, we as a family can participate in the mystery of belief and celebration about creation and Creator. We can share a common faith even though we have experienced it differently. Our worldview here is changing us. It's not an intellectual exercise. It is a matter of heart and soul."

When Jerry finished, there was quiet, many heads nodding. Finally, Gloria looked to Arne and said, "Did you get all of that!?"

Arne replied, "I do believe I did."

ARE YOU LISTENING? 1973 - 1980

A year after the question, "*Kwa nini?*" was asked at Gloria's party, we began to co-direct a teenage street theater group at our church. Using folk tales, poetry, song, and dance from African and African American sources, they spoke, sang, danced, and beat drums. For seven years,

"Are You Listening?" provided an avenue of expression, a common ground for our teenagers who came from many different parts of Durham. I would write the script in story-telling fashion, weaving in expressions of suffering, survival, hope, and love.

"Are You Listening to the beat of the feet, when it's right next to your door, or can you only hear the beat that comes from a far-off shore?" When we sang this song, we alerted our audience to the near and far of the message and the rich resources of the authors.

In the seventies, the names of Langston Hughes, Lance Jeffers, and Miriam Makeba were unknown to many teenagers. "The Simple Tales," "The Power of These Black Hands," and "Mommy" were transformed to life in their song, dance, and voice. Wearing African *dashiki*-style shirts, they were "Wading in the Water" as "Are You Listening?" found a life beyond our church.

Each year, I'd rewrite the script with new material. The power of the message, the heritage and eloquence of the words captured the hearts of those speaking and those listening. We received requests to bring "Are You Listening?" to racism conferences, congregations, and assemblies, sending us all over the Southeast and even to the Midwest. New sounds, new voices, new beats.

What was it that so captured the imaginations of performers and audiences? The power of poetry, the humor of folktale, the eloquence of movement brought the drumbeat of words into new places. Many had never heard of the authors, many had never heard the beats, but many were able to hear the message. With teenagers speaking, singing, and dancing, another transformation took place. The words became flesh.

Kitereza's folktale "*Enkwambu and Enkende*" embodied the core message—all the way from Ukerewe. All the way from this remote island in Lake Victoria where three distinct ethnic groups lived together in close proximity. Difference. Difference in image, in custom, in manner, in possibility. In the profound wisdom of folk literature, the question is asked: what keeps us apart?

I had translated this folktale from Kitereza's book and then adapted it into verse for "Are You Listening?" It made the mime work well. There was a beat. Son Karl was the black-faced monkey, and his black buddy Warrick was the white-faced lizard. It took a while for the audience to get it.

ENKWAMBU AND ENKENDE

A Kerebe folktale by Aniceti Kitereza

I have a little story that I think you will like,
About a monkey who is BLACK and a lizard who is WHITE.
Enkwambu, the monkey, was walking one day
When he met Enkende, the lizard, so he stopped to say –

"Listen, my friend, come to my house and eat –
I promise I'll fix you a very special treat!"
With delight the lizard asked, "When will this be?"
And Enkwambu, the monkey, said – "Tomorrow, I'm free."

The monkey hurried home to tell his wife,
Cause they'd never fed a lizard in their entire life!
The monkey said, "Lizards like intestines of a fish."
His wife said, "You really think THAT'S a tasty dish?"
The monkey said, "I'm off to see our chief, for I'm sure he'll agree
To make our friend the lizard part of our family!"
When the lizard arrived the next day to dine,
Everything was prepared especially fine.
The chair, the table, everything was set –
If only the chief's rules could be easily met!
The monkey said, "Friend, I'm sure you'll agree –
Good friends are just part of one big family!
My chief said you can become one of us
If you'll eat in a chair, without too much fuss!"

So the lizard tried – and he tried – and he tried some more –
But he ALWAYS landed – on the floor!
Sadly, the lizard went home.

Later that week, the monkey was walking one day,
And he met the lizard, who stopped to say –
Listen, my friend, come to MY house and eat –

I promise I'll fix you a VERY special treat!"
With delight the monkey asked, "When will this be?"
Enkende, the lizard, said – "Tomorrow, I'm free."

The lizard hurried home to tell HIS wife,
Cause they'd NEVER fed a monkey in THEIR entire life!
The lizard said, "Monkeys think corn is good food!"
His wife said, "If I told you what I think, you'd say that I'm rude!"
The lizard said, "I'm off to see our chief, for I'm sure he'll agree
To make our friend the monkey part of our family!"
When the monkey arrived the next day to dine,
Everything was prepared especially fine!
The chair, the table, everything was set –
If only the chief's rules could be easily met!
The monkey sat happily, ready to eat
The corn prepared especially as a tasty treat.

The lizard said, "Friend, I'm sure you'll agree –
Good friends are just part of one big family!
My chief said you can become one of us –
Just make your face white – like MINE – without too much fuss!"
So the monkey washed – and he washed – and he scrubbed his face sore,
But alas, he was just as BLACK as before!
Now my friends, it is obvious to see
That God's been very busy, creating you and me!
The question is – DO we belong – to one big family?

"Are You Listening?" ushered us into church spaces where, presumably, we could look at this question in new ways. Our small congregation in Durham, North Carolina, had voices of leadership emerging as well. In the late 1970s, Gloria became the first African American woman to sit on the church council of the American Lutheran Church. Within a few years, Shiela Small, Rosa and Bill's daughter, was elected to the Multicultural Youth Council, a new organization within the national Luther League. We were so proud.

It was newsworthy. Pictures of Shiela appeared in the *Minneapolis Tribune* as well as the *Durham Herald*. Within a few weeks, anonymous letters appeared in the Smalls' mailbox on Tuggle Street in Durham. Word after word, "Stay with your own kind. You don't belong here!"

"WHY?" we all cried. "Why would anyone do such a thing?"

Under closer scrutiny, the Minneapolis postmark screamed, "We're white here. We have our heritage. We have ours, you have yours. Don't come here!"

That was in the seventies. In 2012, I attended a GLOCAL gathering of Lutheran church people in Minneapolis. It's a new word, *glocal*. It acknowledges our interdependence in this twenty-first century global world no matter where we call home. Global and local have less and less space between them.

Kwa nini? Now this question comes to us from another direction. We are not the stranger, the *mgeni*, who is crossing over into someone else's space. Now the *mgeni* is coming nearer and nearer into all our spaces—our neighborhoods, our schools, our hospitals, our work places. And, sometimes, even our churches.

"We send significant dollars to Madagascar," said one GLOCAL participant, "but we're not ready to engage our new neighbors into our church life."

Why?

10 **WAZUNGU** (wahZOONgoo)   pro. *WHITE FOLK*

Throughout the stories in this lexicon, there have been hints if not outright lived examples of how stereotyping others often results in what and where they may go, impeding who they might become. There is nothing new about naming groups of people. The human need to blame, denigrate, and violate for group or self-gain is ageless. It is a process that infiltrates institutions and mindsets, thereby rationalizing and legalizing behaviors that not only give permission to exclude others but to limit their access to a full life. To determine another's worth is to take on god power.

Wazungu is the plural of *mzungu*. It is the collective word for white folk, those for whom privilege, entitlement, and choice are assumed. It is the collective word for those who have used their power to name others' worth. This word turns the in-between space inside out, for we are the ones being translated by those with whom we have chosen to engage.

In many places, here and abroad, our collective identity precedes us with assumptions that we are *missionaries, mercenaries, or misfits*. Furthermore, our collective reputation names us as arrogant, ignorant, domineering, condescending, and greedy, causing some to say "go home" or "give me your money and leave." Whether we are *crackers, gringos,* or *wazungu*, we are now being named out loud with increasing volume and ferocity.

For many well-intentioned *wageni*, there is little understanding of how we are perceived because for many of us, as white majority, the attendant power to name others has been a life- long given. Not only have we written the relational script, we have typecast the players.

84

Furthermore, we are the directors. It can be a crash course in identity stereotyping when we find ourselves in this negative collective space. Emotions of fear, anger, and indignation can be our primary responses. Is it possible to rewrite the script – together?

THE GOOD SAMARITAN 1999

One evening, a Mwangaza volunteer teacher, Jim Talarico, was heading to the Kilimanjaro Airport with our staff driver to await his wife's arrival on the eight p.m. flight from Amsterdam. They left my home in plenty of time, early evening, when it was still light. They weren't taking any chances of not being there when she walked through the final customs gate.

It was about nine p.m. when I was surprised by a *hodi* at my door. Puzzled, as it was too soon for Jim and Sue's return, I hurried to answer. The gentleman greeting me quickly said, "There's been an accident with your Mwangaza car at the junction of Ilboru Road and the Moshi-Nairobi highway."

The word accident all but brought me to my knees. "Is anyone hurt? Jim? Allen?" He hastened to tell me that somehow, the car had landed in a cement culvert to avoid hitting a small child who had darted into the road.

"Where is Jim? Where is Allen?"

"I don't know about Jim. I didn't see him," he replied. "But Allen is there. It might be good if you come with me. I have a car."

As we made our way down the road, my head was in turmoil to say nothing of my heart. What happened? Why hadn't I been notified earlier? The five-minute drive felt like hours. As we neared the intersection, we could see crowds of people gathered around the culvert that still held our Mwangaza car in its grip. Allen stood to the side as several men valiantly tried to leverage our Land Rover up and out, a challenge that for two hours continued to foil all attempts.

Running to his side, my questions tumbled out. "How are you? Were you hurt? Where is Jim? Is he okay?" Allen, our Mwangaza driver, responded by telling me that since the accident, he had stood guard so that the hordes of people swarming to the scene would keep away from the car. When a safari car stopped and asked if they could assist, he told them that Jim's wife was soon arriving. Since the car was headed to the airport, Jim had quickly gotten in, grateful for this Good Samaritan offer.

By eleven p.m., the safari car returned safely with Jim and Sue. The Mwangaza car was finally on the road. Allen and I drove home in wordless exhaustion yet a knowing of gratitude for everyone's well-being.

The next morning, as Jim, Sue, and I prepared to attend the village church service, I suggested that a monetary gift for our Good Samaritan might be appropriate. After church, we all stood for some time, recounting the events with laughter and marveling at this amazing saga.

Later that week, I was surprised to see our Good Samaritan at my doorstep. Delighted to see him again, we sat on the verandah as he began to recount his personal story. "I've been studying at Makumira Seminary," he said, "but I have had to stop due to the drought and lack of funds. With so little rain," he continued, "I've not had the corn crop I anticipated. And this means I am now faced with no funds to pay for my daughter's school fees. I've even sold my cow, but it isn't enough."

It was clear where this was going. However, what impressed me was the concern expressed for his daughter, not for himself. Wanting to know more, I said, "Tell me about your daughter."

With pride, he said, "She's studying math and science at Pugu Secondary School in Dar es Salaam."

Here was a father, a seminarian, trying his best to care for his family and particularly this daughter. Without another thought, I agreed to give him the necessary funds so that she might continue her schooling.

Later that week, a member of our Mwangaza staff came up to me and quietly asked, "Mama, did Daudi come to see you at your home?"

"Oh yes," I replied, and then I relayed his story with no lack of enthusiasm for all he was trying to do amidst so many challenges.

There was a pause and then John said very gently, "Mama, I'm sorry to tell you this. But Daudi is no longer at the seminary. He was dismissed. Furthermore, he had no cow and no daughter in secondary school."

I was speechless in Arusha. Was I a newcomer to Tanzania? Hardly. Was I aware of ongoing scams? Of course. Had I been duped before? Yes, but not with such cunning cleverness. Even though I had never met Daudi before the car accident, he knew enough about me to make his case: a faith woman committed to girls' education.

Later, John and our Mwangaza staff suggested that from then on, when any personal requests came to me, I'd simply defer by saying, "Until I talk with my Mwangaza family, I can't make any decision."

It's a precarious place to be as *wazungu* - this in-between space, where we dare recognize one another, where we dare walk a new walk, accompanying one another not because we ought to but because we have to. This is where forgiveness doesn't leave us on our knees. This is where hope is born as we learn to walk humbly between the words, forging relationships of mutual trust and respect. It is in this transformative space where doing justice, loving kindness, and showing mercy become common life translations.

It's called The Beloved Community.

Forgivenessreconciliation

Needswants

Ethniccreed
Privilegeright

T
H
E   Rightwrong

C   Conservativeliberal
U
T   Justicemercy
T   Sacredsecular
I   Successfailure
N
G
      Securitycertainty

Lifedeath   Goodevil
E
D   Uswe
G   Privatepublic
E

Lovehate

Heavenearth

Choice

11 **UZIMA** (ooZEEmah)   n. *WELLNESS*

It's hard to translate because it takes more than one word to define it. *Uzima* is more than health. *Uzima* speaks to an ever-evolving life condition of heart, mind, and soul. At the core is the One who is life's center. This One may be called many names, *Mungu*-God, *Mtakatifu*-Spirit, *Mungu Mwenyezi*-Creator. There are times, however, when *uzima* is very absent.

ARUSHA **2000**

Cervical cancer is a vicious illness pervasive in Tanzania. Yet pain medication is not easily procured. The cancer robs a woman of *uzima*. Death is slow and excruciatingly painful. Families tire of the endless caretaking for not only is the *mgonjwa*, the sick one, unable to contribute anything to the community, but her illness affects everyone. Fear stalks and caregivers grow weary; there is no relief for anyone. Cries to God are wailed in homes, in villages, and in cities.

When these pain-filled cries are caused by terminal illnesses, there is more than a body affliction that is overwhelming the patient. Hospice is a caring process that acknowledges the need for physical, emotional, psychological, and spiritual solace for the dying. Eight years ago, my son Kristopher moved to Tanzania with his family to assist in the development of hospice care with the Lutheran church in Tanzania. In places like Tanzania, hospice more and more involves those dying from cancer and from HIV/AIDS.

One day, Kristopher was asked by Paulina, a hospice nurse, and Augustine, the evangelist, if he could join them on their next visit to a woman suffering with cervical cancer. Several months earlier, Paulina had walked the ten miles to visit Rachel, but now their schedules did not permit a return unless a car could be found. As our Mwangaza car was available, Paulina insisted that I accompany their team. It was an experience I will always treasure because of its searing rawness and its blinding beauty.

When we arrived at the *boma*, Rachel's home, two daughters ran to greet us, anxious to tell Paulina the latest news about their mama's health. Rachel had been bedridden for months, wracked in pain. They were weary of her wails, and they were weary of their inability to soothe her.

We were ushered into a very dark room; only a small, shuttered window let in a thin shaft of light. Rachel lay on the bed, a still form. Paulina went to her bedside, quietly greeting her. Taking Rachel's hand in hers, she began to stroke her arm as she asked, "How are you? How have these days been since I last saw you?"

Paulina's soothing touch and words gradually unleashed a torrent of words, words of pain, words of fear, words of God, where are you? The dark room began to fill with her anguish. The words were everywhere; they were stuck on the walls; they hung from the ceiling. I felt them circling around Rachel's bed, these words that encrusted not only the endless pain of her body but also of her heart.

Fear. As Paulina listened, as all of us listened, the words began to diminish in size as she was able, finally, to give them away, able to give them to someone who understood. Someone who was not a daughter. Someone who was not her husband. Someone who could absorb the words.

When the tidal wave ebbed, Paulina said, "Rachel, I have brought you friends. You see at the end of the bed is an *mzungu* doctor. *Jina lake ni* Kristopher. His name is Kristopher. He is here to help you. And next to me, this is his mama, Mama Shoonie. And over there, is *Mwinjlisti* Augustine."

There was still quiet from Rachel. Slowly she moved her head to face Paulina. "An *mzungu* doctor to see me with his mama?"

Paulina responded in her quiet tone, "Yes, they are here to see you."

At that moment, Kristopher quietly moved to sit by Rachel on her bed. He took her hand in his and said very, oh, so very quietly, "*Pole, Rachel. Najua unauma sana. Sema, tu.* I am so sorry, Rachel. I know you are hurting badly. Tell me."

For a moment, Rachel seemed stunned to speechlessness, but it was momentary. The words began to tumble out as her voice found itself once again. When she finished, it was as if her energy was spent with the telling. There was quiet in the room. Kristopher explained to her that the medicine he would give her would help relieve her pain. He explained, oh, so quietly, that this medicine wouldn't take it away completely. But he hoped and prayed that she would find some relief. Throughout, he held her hand.

Silence filled the room as Rachel absorbed it all. And then from Augustine, the evangelist, who had been sitting quietly in the dark, listening, came a murmur, a hum, a tune. Let me describe Augustine. His shirt was buttoned askew. His shoelaces were untied. You might think, because of his appearance, that Augustine was not fully present. Or, you might think, because of his rather rough-shod appearance, that he was a bit out of place and didn't quite fit with a doctor and a hospice nurse.

In the quiet of this dark, pain-filled room, a voice began softly, "*Mungu ni pendo.*" It was Augustine singing this beloved hymn, "God is love." Within moments, we were all joining him, Kristopher in his sweet tenor, Paulina's rich alto below my quavering soprano. The three of us were led by this tender evangelist whose manner was exactly what was needed. This humble man of God had created a healing space for Rachel's spirit. When we finished singing, he prayed. He prayed for her rest in the arms of Jesus, for her peace in the heart of God. *Uzima.*

A few weeks later, Paulina was able to visit Rachel again. Her daughters could not say enough about the effect of the medicine, the change since our visit.

When Paulina asked, "Rachel, how are you?"

A very quiet voice replied, "I am well." *Uzima.*

Soul sickness comes with fear, fear of abandonment, fear of the unknown, fear of being alone, fear of being unloved. *Uzima* comes with being content, knowing how much is enough, loving what you have, and knowing you are loved. For this, there's no insurance policy.

Only faith.

THE DOOR

Gotta' go through
    Can't go round
    Can't go under
    Can't go over
    Gotta' go through
                At the door
    Abraham's bosom
    Cradling all God's children

The room is dark
    One small window cracked
        Sliver
            Shaft of light

    Reveals the shrinking body
        Of a woman
            Waiting
                Waiting for Paulina to come
                Paulina to touch
                    Paulina to listen

    Cervical cancer wracks her body
        Pain rips the wretched flesh
            Year   after   Year

    Augustin   compassionate evangelist
        Sits quietly   watching
    Kristopher   gentle doctor
        Sits quietly   listening

As this woman tells of the waiting

        Paulina's name is incanted
        A litany
            For it is she who comes
                It is she who touches
                It is she who listens

It is she
    Who brings us

    Through the door

Mungu ni pendo we sing
God is love

Augustin prays
Kristopher medicates
Paulina soothes

The bosom of Abraham enfolds

As Sarah rocks

You gotta' go thru

At

The

Door

What does hunger look like?

Samaki ~ Bahati

SAMAKI **2008**

You might call it a fishy business. The Nile perch was introduced into Lake Victoria's aquaculture in the late 1800s. It set in motion a downward spiral of ecological imbalance. An aggressively predatory fish, *samaki*, the Nile perch has now consumed nearly every other species in the lake, growing to enormous size in the process. With the overabundance of this voracious fish, there is famine, there is *njaa*. There is an imbalance between the dominating perch and the smaller fish that ate algae and waste to maintain the water's purity.

The second largest fresh-water lake in the world, Lake Victoria is shared by Uganda, Kenya, and Tanzania. For as long as memory records, its waters have been a food resource for multitudes and an income generator for local fisherman. Now, not only has the insatiable hunger of the Nile perch drastically lowered native fish populations, the effect on people in the countries bordering the lake is horrific.

The appetites of the Nile perch are matched by consumer demand for fish in Europe and elsewhere. International airlines fly into Mwanza, the Lake Victoria port city in Tanzania, to transport fillets of Nile perch to people with esoteric palates and deep pockets in other parts of the world. It's a lucrative business. But it is deadly, particularly for the women and children who prepare the perch for export under dangerous conditions for subsistence wages.

The portion of the fish carcass that remains after filleting is undesirable for export and is left behind. Yet even these scraps are too expensive for local Tanzanians. The rate of prostitution in this region is one of the highest in the country. The streets are overflowing with orphaned children. The incidence of HIV/AIDS is skyrocketing.

"If the world were a Global Village of one hundred inhabitants" is a reminder of who we are:

60 would be Asian, 14 African, 12 European, 8 Latin American, 5 US/Canadian

82 would be non-white

67 would be non-Christian

80 would live in sub-standard housing

67 would be unable to read

50 would be malnourished

1 would have a college education

7 would have access to the internet

5 U.S. citizens would control 32% of all the world's wealth

33 would attempt to live on only 3% of the total income

The ethics of Ghandi's list of the seven deadly sins addresses the *njaa* balance:

Wealth without work

Enjoyment without conscience

Knowledge without character

Business without morality

Science without humanity

Religions without sacrifice

Politics without principle

Samaki. Njaa. Fish, hunger, prostitution, orphans, poverty, disease. Is it possible to imagine a balance between those who have too much of what they want and those who have too little of what they need? Is it possible to even imagine living life abundantly, wherever we are?

A scriptural response: "The one who had much did not have too much and the one who had little did not have too little." II Corinthians 8: 13-15.

THE LORD IS MY SHEPHERD

I have all I need

Her body is tall, lean, gracefully elegant
    Silver bracelets encircle her wrists
    Her ringed ankles echo her measured tread

Draped in robes of purple and red
    Ears pierced
    Chest plate
        adorned in colored beads

She walks with regal gait
    Her crown
    A bucket steadied
    Unerringly
    On her head

        She has all she needs

She walks
    Precious water
    One bucket

        She has all she needs

Eight kilometers she walks
Meeting other women
    One bundle of firewood
    One stack of banana leaves
    Unerringly
    On their heads

Mama takwenya   they greet in Maa
    Iko

Don't break the tread
She eases past as she greets

        She has all she needs

Don't stumble
Don't spill

        She bears her day's needs

          The Lord is my shepherd
               I need all I want

          To be Number One

Help me
I don't understand

She's there
I'm here
        What is needful

            To live life

               Abundantly?

            The Lord is our shepherd

          Do we have

      All

        We

         Need?

BAHATI 1999

I didn't know her name when I first saw her. A scrawny, tattered toddler. She would run to the road each morning when she heard the cranking up of my diesel four-wheel drive heading to Mwangaza.

One day, hearing a *hodi* at my door, I found this little one with her parents. She clung to her mama's *khanga*, hiding behind her. She didn't look at me. Scared. Trembling. It was probably the closest she'd been to a white mama. After the greetings, her parents explained that they wished to have their daughter baptized at our Ilboru church. But she didn't have a dress, well, not a nice one. Might I consider helping?

In the list of endless requests, this was easy. On the day of her baptism, the family came to my door, her mama proudly displaying her daughter in a frilly blue organdy ankle-length dress. She could wear it for years. Shoes barely hanging onto her little feet. Maybe she'd grow into them in three years?

Yet no adornment could change her reality. She lived in sub-standard housing. Undoubtedly her daily diet was inadequate. Sanitation? In the global village list, her life and those of her family members were riddled with *njaa*.

Gradually, we began to communicate. As I'd brake the car on the hill each morning, I'd wave to her, not a big hand motion, just a little one. For weeks, she'd stand at attention, no acknowledgement, no smile. But always there. Then, one day, one little hand started to twitch at her side. A beginning? Little by little, her hand would move into a wave until one day, there was even a smile. A game?

Let's play. So began a mime exchange. As I'd hold onto the steering wheel, I'd give her some finger motions. Eyes bright, a smile, she brought her hands up, looked at them, looked at me and played back. Every morning, we did this. As time went by and her little brother could toddle, there were two racing to the roadside, ready for finger play.

Our Ilboru Church had a pre-school program right across the road from Mwangaza. One day her *baba* came to see me. Might I consider tuition for this daughter? Education. The dream of parents world-wide is that it might just make the difference, the possibility that the global list would not be their children's fate. Education could stave off *njaa*.

That was ten years ago. This little girl is growing into a beautiful young woman and proudly shows me her school reports from secondary school. An unimagined dream now has possibility.

There is a documentary chronicling the Nile perch and its attendant disasters. It is well named—*Darwin's Nightmare*. This young girl is also well named. She is *Bahati*. It means luck.

THE WHIRLWIND

The whirlwind roars
    To bare Moses' feet
        To part seas
            To scatter possessions
                To witness crucifixions

The whirlwind's quiet
    As women wail
        Children weep
            Homeless wander
                Disease overwhelms

The whirlwind circles
    Voices of greed
        Insatiable possessing
            Sunday security
                Militaristic materialism

The whirlwind blows
    Life to Sarah
        And Hagar?
    Hope to Hannah
        And Tamar?
    Privilege to David
        And Bathsheba?
    Protection to men
        And women?

The whirlwind enfolds
    Job's goodness
        Who loses all
    Mary's magnificat
        Whose son dies
    Jesus' obedience
        Whose love births forgiveness
            And
                Hope

The whirlwind
    Can't be tamed
    Can't be named
    Can't be known

        Knows no beginning
        No end

        IS

Dare we enter this Force
    Of Being
        Where we've always been

    Daring the whirlwind to explode its
    Mysteries
    And
        Possibilities

Whirling our feet to the desert
    Our hands to the maimed
        Our eyes to the pulsing vortex

    Of

    Light

13 **ASANTE / SHUKRANI** (ahSAHNtey / shooKRAHnee)
v. *THANK YOU / GRATITUDE*

For a small word, *asante* has more running room than any other. No matter the language, thank you acknowledges that we have received something of value, a gift, a gesture, a welcome. *Shukrani* is lived gratitude. In places like Tanzania, it is startling in its interpretations.

MAGDALENA 1999

An ancient woman taught me a profound lesson, one that continues to sustain me. I first saw her at church on a Sunday morning. The Ilboru congregation had built a large cement church near the one where I had learned to sing way back in the sixties. We had outgrown that space and already, we were over-crowded in the new. By the time the pastor started his sermon, most of the wooden benches were filled to capacity.

This old woman always arrived late. I first noticed her clothing. She wore a grey hooded Michigan sweatshirt over an organdy prom-like skirt. Oversized tennis shoes with frog-green socks scrunched around her ankles completed her ensemble. She shuffled as she walked down the aisle, her back bowed over from many years' toil on her *shamba*, or farm. Her purse almost dragged on the ground. Perching on the end of a plank bench, she joined in the chorus "*Furahia, Furahia, Wakristo.* Rejoice, Rejoice People of God/Christ." And I wondered. Just what does she have to be thankful for?

Sunday after Sunday, she would come late, moving slowly, carefully sitting on the end of the bench and then joining in the service. I had noticed her long enough. I asked a friend, Samweli, if he would find out what he could about her.

104

"She lives right across the road," he said. "Her name is Magdalena. She's a widow, living alone in a lean-to shack, relying on village children to beg for her. She is really very, very poor. There is no family living near-by to care for her."

Samweli and I talked about what could be done. As a result, we put together a small packet of rice, beans, tea, soap, and sugar. I suggested that he say it was a gift from church. When he returned the next day, he told me more about her story.

"She has been a widow for many years," he said. "None of her sons live nearby and her daughters are with their families up the mountain. Last night, when she built a small fire and cooked her last greens, her *khanga*, her cotton wrap, caught on fire. She slapped her leg until the fire went out and she thanked God for being spared.

As I gave her the food, she shook her head in wonder and said, "Now you come, unbidden, with this gift. Let me go to church and give thanks."

Although I had asked Samweli to tell her that the small packet was from church, when Magdalena saw me the next Sunday, she waved. As she continued hesitatingly, making her way down the aisle, she broke into a broad smile revealing her toothless gums. Several days later, she appeared at our Mwangaza gate. Seelah, one of our staff, greeted her and then looking to me, she asked, "Magdalena, do you know this mama?"

Magdalena took my hand in hers and said, "Only through God."

Magdalena became our Mwangaza *Koko*, our Mwangaza Grandmother. Every month, she slowly wended her way down the mountain path, steadied by her makeshift cane. She sat on our verandah and patiently waited for *chai* and her small packet of monthly supplies. One of her daughters had died from AIDS; others in the family were ill.

Magdalena was like many women her age in Tanzania. She was the caretaker for her family. She represented the gap between parent and children, where there are grandparents, but no parents, where there are increasing numbers of children abandoned and orphaned. Children who are desperate for care and love.

105

Where there is scarcity, it's amazing the abundance within *asante*. No cup of *chai*, tea, no bowl of *uji*, porridge, no plate of *wali na maharage*, beans and rice, no *safari*, trip, safely ended escapes this response. It goes not only to the giver but to the spiritual source as well. Daily happenings are peppered with this acknowledgement. *Asante* is the binding thread woven into all aspects of daily life, a wellspring of bounty.

It isn't difficult to say *asante*. *Shukrani,* on the other hand, is an attitude, a way of life. Thanksgiving for a day, gratitude for the moment is a way of being. *Shukrani* is in every place, in every situation, in every person. *Shukrani* is an ongoing revelation of *Mungu* presence. A life-living discovery.

This is Magdalena, *Baraka wa Mungu*, our continuing, our ageless Blessing from God.

Thanksgiving

Pain is missed in praise

It's the only time
    I've disagreed
        With Emily
            Dickenson
                that is

But then if she'd been here
        Where pain is not missed in praise

Not like at home
    Where we work so very hard
        To walk on top of pain
        To deny suffering

    Ignore it away
    Drink it away
    Exercise it away
    Praise it away

When praise is on a grid of answers

                No
            Questions

        Not a Rilke response

When faith knows but dares not feel
    When faith knows but denies vulnerability
        When faith knows but insists on its on our way

God forgive us

    For then
    From what source is
        Our praise
            Our healing
                Our thanksgiving

Here
    Pain is part of praise
    Sorrow is part of joy
    Life is part of death
    Mystery is part of revelation

      Nospaces

Except for the gouged valleys
Except for thanksgiving
      Erupting out of the depths

      Of pain
      Not missed
      In praise

      Shukrani
      Thanksgiving

      For
    Seeing the face of God
    One
         More
    Day

      For

    A safe journey
    Every morsel of food
    Rain

      For

    A malaria cure
    A healed relationship
    A book

Pain is so searing   Praise is so exultant
    Nothing is missed

      In
    Praise

14 **SIRI** (SEEree)   n. *MYSTERY, SECRET*

It would be so much easier if *Education of a Stranger* provided *Steps of Awareness* for the crossing-over traveler, or better yet, a clear-cut *Stranger Etiquette Guide*. More importantly, there would be no ambiguity, no questions. Like a good recipe, the ingredients would be measured in exact proportions including the process of how to assemble the parts to make a whole. It would be clearly stated. The best part would be a guarantee that if you followed directions, if you did all the right things and, very especially, if you baked it at just the proper degree and for the required time, the outcome could be guaranteed: A well-seasoned stranger.

Instead, I have walked with you into many different spaces; I have introduced you to many different people. Throughout, the underlying meanings, unexplained possibilities await translation. They wait for us to unfold, to uncover our own interpretations. They await our lived answers to the questions: Why should we stand between the words and dare to go inside? What difference does it make?

All the difference in the world. If there were only one song to sing, one book to read, one landscape to see, one voice to hear, how unimaginably dull life would be. The plethora of worldviews, people, places, and expressions is breathtaking. We can learn to appreciate and even to understand at some level how it is that others live as they do. But when we really get into the translations of your and my way of being, that requires us to enter words of suffering and celebration, of exclusion and acceptance, of hatred and love; this is where secret revelations await new translations.

These life reality words we all know. And it is in this space, as *wageni*, where we recognize one another more clearly. It is in this space where we can be available to a new presence within life's mysteries that will not only sustain us but cause us to discover, together, renewed strength for the common good—that we might all live life abundantly.

It can make all the difference
Crossing over

Amri zako zimekuwa nyimbo zangu katika nyumba ya ugeni.
Zaburi 119:54

into this in-between space

where mystery unfolds

where *Mungu* God is so startling

where *Mungu* God is so hidden

in every *where*

in every face

in every lived

word

where

justice   kindness   reconciliation

wait

Mungu Mystery

Mungu Promise

Mungu

Presence

Your statutes have been my song wherever I have lived as a stranger.

Psalm 119:54

Namshukuru Mungu

A STRANGER'S CANTICLE

Blessed are you who dare to walk off the map
For the world will be opened unto you

Blessed are you who have *njaa*
For your hunger will never be satisfied

Blessed are you who risk not knowing
For your learning will birth new life

Blessed are you who meet at the Cross roads
Upendo wa Mungu will sustain you

Blessed are You   Source of all Light
Your Love of all Creation
Transforms us

REFLECTIONS

- Describe your beginning understanding of each word.
- What are the causes of change in word understanding?
- What are the global/local implications in each word?
- What ethical dilemmas or challenges are revealed in each word?
- What is your response to the tensions between the *I* and the *We*?
- How do issues of gender, culture, and economics challenge the stranger?
- In what ways does one's belief system affect word life and meaning?
- What issues are raised for advocacy? What emotions are expressed?
- What meaning is between the lines and inside these words?
- Why should we cross over into that in-between space and dare enter the words?
- Describe a common good for which you would cross thresholds, and why.

ABOUT THE AUTHOR

For over 50 years, Shoonie Hartwig has been crossing thresholds – as a coordinator for a student exchange program between Lutheran colleges and the University of Dar es Salaam, Tanzania; as a researcher on the island of Ukerewe, Tanzania; as a mission facilitator with Mwangaza Education for Partnership ELCT/ELCA; as a member of predominantly African American congregations; and as a writer.

39038933R00075

Made in the USA
Lexington, KY
06 February 2015